MW00684936

MECHANICS
of a
POLICE
INTERNAL
AFFAIRS
INVESTIGATION

Robert A. Verry

Looseleaf
Law Publications, Inc.

43-08 162nd Street
Flushing, NY 11358
www.LooseleafLaw.com
800-647-5547

Library of Congress In-Publication Data

Verry, Robert A.
  Mechanics of a police internal affairs investigation / Robert A. Verry.
     p. cm.
  ISBN 978-1-932777-97-0
  1. Police misconduct--United States. 2. Police--Complaints against--United States. 3. Police internal investigation--United States. I. Title.
  HV8139.V47 2011
  363.2'2--dc22

1st Printing, 2011
2nd Printing, 2013

2010047347

The author recognizes the contribution of the female officer in the police service. It is only for ease of reading that the masculine pronoun is used herein.

Cover by *Sans Serif,* Saline, Michigan

Dedication

It is easy to be there for someone when everything is going great, but it takes a special person to be there for you when times are tough. The three inspirational people in my life who were there for me when times were tough are my maternal grandmother, my mother, and my wife; therefore, I dedicate this book to them.

Table of Contents

About the Author

ROBERT A. VERRY started his career with the Middlesex County College Police Department in 1988, joining South Bound Brook Police Department in 1989. He served as P.B.A. President before being promoted to Sergeant in 1995; Lieutenant in 1996; Chief in 2000; and retiring in March 2008. Presently, Robert is a full-time Assistant Professor of American Political & Governmental Affairs with Centenary College. His courses are related to Leadership and Public Administration in the Masters program; Political & Governmental Affairs and Criminal Justice in the Bachelors program.

Since 2007, Robert has provided law enforcement consulting services throughout New Jersey and while in that capacity served as a Hearing Officer for sworn and unsworn personnel, reviewed police departments' internal affairs policy and procedures, reviewed defense experts' reports, and served as an investigator. He qualified and testified as an expert in Superior Court specifically for: *Internal Affairs and Supervisory Investigations, Policies, and Procedures.*

Robert earned an Associate's in Liberal Arts, a Bachelor's in Sociology / Criminal Justice, and a Master's in Leadership and Public Administration all from Centenary College. Additionally, he is a graduate Paralegal from Fairleigh Dickenson University as well as a Certified Public Manager and a graduate of West Point Command & Leadership, Public Sector Labor Relations Certificate Program, and Police Law Enforcement Executive. Furthermore, he is a certified instructor in Crash Investigation I, Crash Investigation II, Vehicle Dynamics, a Master Instructor in RADAR, and Occupant Protection Usage & Enforcement and a Crash Reconstructionist. He possesses certifications in Horizontal Gaze Nystagmus, Traffic Engineering [from Rutgers], and Methods of Instruction.

Robert is the founding member of *New Jersey's Internal Affairs Association* and has served as its president since the 2004 commencement. He has been directly and indirectly involved in well over 1,000 police misconduct investigations and has presented over 100 seminars across New Jersey related to Internal Affairs investigations including, but not limited to, a basic course that reviews the Attorney General Internal Affairs Policy and Procedure, Employee Discipline, Understanding Past Practice, and Controlling Absenteeism.

Introduction

This book is written to offer a practical, not legal (I am not an attorney), guide to some of the most common allegations faced today. It will assist in leveling the playing field of not only the internal affairs investigator and target officer, but also the legal advisors, the victims of police misconduct, the unions, and every potential target law enforcement officer (i.e., every officer).

Most officers reluctantly accept the unpleasant and undesirable assignment of investigating the suspected misconduct of one of their own. The newly assigned investigator goes in knowing that investigating a person who wears a blue uniform cannot be compared to any other kind or type of investigation, and the outcome in most cases will be based on who is the cat and who is the mouse. That is to say, when both the internal affairs investigator and target officer are both educated in Federal and State laws and equally well trained and skilled in such things as interrogation, deceptiveness, and undercover operations, then who is the cat or mouse changes with each move, similar to a game of chess.

An excellent investigator, who wants to remain the cat, plans his actions in advance and calculates his target's reactions. At the same time the target officer strategically attempts to learn as much as he can first-hand or through the assistance of his colleagues and union officials. It is this lawful clever manipulation that makes each move so intriguing. The chapters that follow offer some beneficial tools all parties can use to better understand the means to the end. Those means touch on what an investigator should be concerned with as well as what the target officers should be cognizant of.

Just as members of the department believe the mission of an internal affairs investigator is to find fault, a new internal affairs investigator takes the assignment thinking the same thing. However, both could not be further from the truth. Remaining neutral is optimum, but an investigator needs to go into the investigation uncovering legitimate grounds to find in favor of the officer. To put it another way, the investigator should examine the facts, statements, and evidence from the defense's standpoint, not the agencies. This method of handling an investigation gives the internal affairs investigator the ability to find the supervisor's and department's flaws (e.g., procedural and otherwise) with the case, and lets him determine whether or not those flaws are too fatal to warrant the filing of charges (i.e., if the investigator can find the flaws so can the target officer's defense attorney). Accordingly, for an investigator to maintain his impartiality throughout the entire process, he needs to be impartial to all sides even though he answers directly to the Chief Law Enforcement Officer. As such, it is not the investigator's job to take the side of the agency or target officer; it is the investigator's job to uncover the truth: nothing more; nothing less.

Regardless of how impartial the investigator truly is, most target officers and union officials will have a difficult time avoiding an adversarial role; however, for all intents and purposes, a fair and just internal affairs investigation should be anything but adversarial and the chapters within were written from all viewpoints. This independent stance is necessary when internal affairs investigators today are proactively putting their officers under endless examination for any departmental, civil, and criminal wrongdoing, thus, drastically changing the way they operated even a decade ago. That is, investigators are no longer sitting back and waiting for a complainant; instead, they are now actively and regularly testing the integrity of their officers. Further-more, investigators are now closely analyzing the once-treated separate acts of suspected misconduct for likely patterns (e.g., officer is out sick every other Monday) or early warning signs (e.g., officer hits parked cars at night while on patrol, a sign he may be falling asleep at the wheel) that could be useful toward the prevention of any potential wrongdoing. In addition to internal affairs investigators, with sub-ordinates nowadays all too often suing their police superiors, the officer's supervisors are now taking a more active role in recognizing policy violations and swiftly addressing what in the past they would have clearly overlooked or blatantly ignored.

The chapters should be read in order the very first time; however, once you do that the book should be placed on your shelf with your collection of reference materials as it is written to also be used as a guide, depending on what type and kind of investigation is being conducted. Furthermore, while the lending of books is great for the borrower, with Murphy's Law that "Anything that can go wrong, will go wrong," you probably should not keep this book too far out of reach.

Through your reading you will also notice that the male pronoun is used throughout only because it makes for an easier read and is meant to indicate both male and female genders.

Lastly, anyone reviewing the index should pick up on the fact that the chapters included only scratch the surface with regards to the mechanics of an internal affairs investigation, for which I offer the following:

(1) Regardless of your role in an internal affairs investigation you should know that the unique particulars surrounding an individual case are impossible to pinpoint without first knowing the exact fact patterns of each case; therefore, digging any deeper would be more of a disservice than a service, and

(2) With regards to the missing chapters (e.g., drug testing, domestic violence, use of force, whistle-blowers, etc.), it is noteworthy to point out they are still being written, so stay tuned.

Therefore, in light of the above please take notice that should you have any procedural (not legal) questions, I am in the background and make myself available for you at BobVerry@aol.com/ www.BobVerry.com.

Chapter 1
Crossing the Rubicon

Causes of Police Misconduct

Understanding some direct causes as to why police officers cross the Rubicon from honesty, integrity, and an ethical reputation to dishonesty, questionable integrity, and corruption is important in later understanding the make-up of the officers under investigation; hereinafter referred to as "Target" officers.

Unfortunately, as will be discussed later, it is not uncommon for supervisors to take a see no evil, speak no evil, and hear no evil approach to addressing bad apples. But even when the department's Chief Law Enforcement Officer (hereinafter "Chief") and the ranking members of his staff proactively correct unacceptable behavior, officers still have taken the slippery slope into unlawful activities.

There are many books, articles, and blogs written on this topic; however, most explanations (if not all) could be narrowed down to just seven direct causes. Over one hundred years ago, Frederick Rogers described the seven causes as, "the Seven Deadly Sins represent the vices which from the beginning of time have made havoc of the noblest aspirations of humanity."[1] Unfortunately societies' noblest do not exclude our law enforcement professionals from these vices, and if or when they create havoc it is many times directed at the people they serve. Over the years the seven have been defined and applied in many different ways and several different forms, but here the seven will be defined in the simplest of terms as it relates specifically to the law enforcement professional. The seven are: Apathy, Gluttony, Greed, Lust, Pride, Resentment, and Wrath.

(1) **Apathy:** Active officers who proactively perform their jobs make no more in salary than their co-workers who are inactive and barely respond to calls when dispatched. The job, when looked at as nothing more than a paycheck, transforms a proactive officer into an apathetic one bringing with him laziness, a decline in motivation, and an officer that will aggressively seek ways to passively perform in a substandard manner. Adding to the cause of an officer's apathy is the fact that a proactive officer will logically experience a far higher

---

[1]   Rogers, Frederick, *The Seven Deadly Sins*, A.H. Bullen, 1907, page 2.

1

citizen and supervisory complaint ratio than an officer who does nothing more than watch grass grow.

Example: Signs of apathy can be seen in reduced ticket production, a decrease in arrests, incidental mistakes on police reports (e.g., current date in box where person's date of birth belongs), and failure to follow the departmental rules (at first unnoticed, but more apparent over time). Interestingly, the whispers regarding this officer's way of behaving will more than likely start from his own coworkers than from his union officials; and if unaddressed long enough, his defiance will become more apparent to those several layers above him.

(2) **Gluttony:** An officer's unfettered ability to sometimes take excessively without paying or being questioned—much more than that one person could possibly use, which surpasses waste. This officer believes he is entitled to it even though in reality he does not even want it; therefore, he continually takes, and takes, and takes purely because in his mind he earned it through his uniform and his position of authority in society. What is interesting about this behavior is that it could be initially learned lawfully depending on the officer's surroundings (e.g., officer attends police-expo where the vendors encourage attendees to take in excess items on display, but once put in their bags the items stay there until they are thrown away). Taking excessively with the end result of throwing away is troubling when what the officer takes is linked to the job.

Example: Gluttony starts simply with an extra-large cup of coffee when he only drinks a small and he ends up throwing the rest out, or he orders an entire pizza pie instead of slices only eats two slices of the eight. While the excessive taking begins with a cup of coffee or pizza pie, it has the potential of getting out of control; e.g., officer uses MasterBadge (i.e., inappropriately flashing a badge to obtain a benefit) to get an upgraded hotel room, first-class seats on an airplane, entrance to a theme park for his family or 10% off purchases at a home improvement store. A common theme running through each of the examples is that in all likelihood he would never have asked for the benefits if not for his belief the badge entitled him to upgrades or extras he really did not need and, in most cases, want.

Fascinatingly, until an officer is refused and the refusal becomes insulting to the officer ("how dare you refuse me" and "do you know who I am?"), this officer's behavior can go undetected for years if not his entire career.

(3) **Greed:** An unwatched, tempted, and trusted officer who outside the job deals with the common day stresses by putting themselves above everyone else both visually (e.g., buys a Hummer, but can only afford a Hyundai) and verbally (e.g., talks a talk they cannot walk). Although gluttony deals with waste of all things and wasting for the sake of nothing more than entitlement, greed attaches to an officer's position in society such as their financial status or their authority in society. It is here where officers, not wanting to be financially inferior to their co-workers, neighbors, family, or friends, have placed greed for the material things above their pride regardless of how their quest for this wealth comes about. While all the sins are objectionable, they are more objectionable when a law enforcement officer is involved. Greed is the most egregious because it involves meticulous action from the officer with a full awareness of his misdeeds. Furthermore, as soon as an officer crosses the Rubicon there's no turning back, and an internal affairs investigator in most cases could and should trace the officer's footprints by following the money, rumors, and lifestyle.

Example: Police officer with open financial troubles stops a car and the driver complains to internal affairs that the money in the glove box is missing; homeowner files a complaint that same officer was in his house on a fireworks complaint and now money and jewelry are missing from his bureau; drug dealer after being arrested by narcotics detectives claims he is constantly shaken down by the same officer for all his cash to avoid being arrested.

An officer's private financial status should have no effect on an officer's employer/employee relationship. But if there is a reason to believe an officer is using his position to directly or indirectly obtain a financial benefit he is not lawfully entitled to, it would be remiss of the internal affairs unit to not investigate further. Additionally, if the officer visually lives a lifestyle beyond his means an investigation may be warranted. However, the investigator needs to tread lightly in these areas and legal advice should be sought before any investigation begins.

(4) **Lust:** The uniform, power, and opportunity are an excellent combination that aid in an officer's sexual appetite for the desire of multiple partners. Although sometimes the partners are willing, a form of lust manifests itself in an unwilling victim who is molested on a traffic stop, unlawfully stripped searched or sexually assaulted on a burglary call. Whether a willing partner or not, when the act takes place when the officer is on duty it than becomes necessary for the officer to cover up what he did.

Example: Female motorist files a complaint with internal affairs that officer groped her on a traffic stop; officer uses department's phone or computer to hook up with sexual partners; married officer asks co-workers to cover for him (e.g., "Tell my (spouse) I'm working overtime and tied up on a call"), while his private vehicle is inconspicuously parked in the area of a house where the officer is frequently observed while on duty.

(5) **Pride:** Pride categorically takes center stage for all other sins as it is pride that influences apathy, gluttony, greed, lust, resentment, and wrath.

Taking control is a necessary course of action officers must employ on most calls, therefore, when on-duty, it places them in a position of superiority. Although this attribute is essential for survival on calls, outside the calls the needless domination should stop. It is when the officer cannot separate himself from being more powerful than all others around him and he is no longer able to recognize unsworn citizens' positive attributes. Sadly, he finds it impossible to separate himself from when it is appropriate to be authoritative and when it is not.

Undisputedly, police officers are police officers 24 hours a day 7 days a week; however, what many police officers lose sight of is that they are human beings first. That is, a police officer puts his pants on one leg at a time just like everyone else. Although there are many times an officer needs to be authoritative and prove he is in control, at the end of the day the officer needs to metaphorically leave his gun belt in his locker. Taking the mightier-than-thou attitude outside the appropriate work setting emotionally creates an unfitting "us versus them" way of thinking. This attitude, at times, does not stop at the officer's home threshold and over time serves as a factor in domestic violence incidents, child and parental abuse, and family and friend relationship terminations.

(6) **Resentment:** I want, what I want, when I want it—even if that includes crossing the Rubicon to get it. But it is not until all is lost that the officer finally realizes that he did not know what he actually had until it was too late. In 2005 the Fort Lauderdale Police Department "disciplined an officer for accepting a free salad from Wendy's fast food restaurant"[2]; a New Jersey officer was arrested [and later acquitted] for allegedly taking a $1.59 nutrition bar; and a California officer was arrested on suspicion of selling meth. While the latter arrest would seem more corrupt, all had the potential of causing the officers to lose their jobs, pay a fine, lose their freedom, and never work in law enforcement again.

On a smaller scale, but certainly not any less immoral, officers, needing to be promoted, have been caught cheating on promotional exams (e.g., recently in San Antonio Texas "[t]hirteen patrol officers will be disciplined ... into allegations of improper conduct during a promotion exam"[3]) and police applicants over the years have certainly looked at their neighbors' tests when they did not know the answer.

(7) **Wrath:** The building up of uncontrolled anger or hatred that presents itself in either a self-destructive way (e.g., suicide, alcoholic, drug abuse) or revenge (e.g., homicide, property damage, unlawful arrests or summonses). The built-up anger, hauntingly, can take years to fester. Sometimes the only reason a person becomes a police officer is because he or she was bullied in elementary school and now seek revenge through newfound authority. While this displaced anger (e.g., kicking the dog because you lost your keys) is sometimes discovered through the police psychologist in the pre-hiring examination, many times it is not disclosed until someone takes notice of an officer's out of place activities (e.g., arresting a female pedestrian for jaywalking because his female Sergeant gave him a Performance Notice or conducting traffic stops only on the race of the motorist, because the bully in elementary school was of that race).

---

[2] http://weblogs.sun-sentinel.com/news/politics/broward/blog/2009/12/police_officials_respond_to_ne.html

[3] http://www.policeone.com/police-jobs/articles/2363068-Texas-promotion-exam-cheating-scandal-ends/

Interestingly, regardless of which one of the above is the driving force behind an officer's misdeeds, most often it is not the initial action or inaction that ends up being the officer's downfall. Rogue police officers will spend countless hours trying to figure out how to cover up their transgressions instead of just doing the right thing. Apparently misguided, misdirected, or just plain foolish, it is not uncommon for a target officer who is under investigation to provide false statements to the internal affairs investigator in an attempt to conceal what they're under investigation for. Targets have also resorted to creating diversions, planting evidence, tampering with witnesses, and various other unthinkable deeds they never would have done if not for the investigation or their need to hide their unethical or criminal actions.

If not for the many deceptive officers' maneuvers during an active investigation, it is highly probable that most police officers fired today would not have lost their jobs. Like François de La Rochefoucauld's quote points out, "Almost all our faults are more pardonable than the methods we think up to hide them,"[4] and too often all an officer had to do was admit his wrongdoings and accept a reasonable penalty; however, once an officer misleads or attempts to deceive an investigator, the target officer's law enforcement career must be terminated.

Kinds of Police Misconduct

There are several types of police misconduct the internal affairs investigator needs to be familiar with. While the few listed below are a small sampling, they are probably the most common.

(1) **Absenteeism:** The allure of being a police officer seems to wear off eventually, with a chosen few who would rather spend more time figuring out how not to come to work than they do figuring out what to do when they are at work. Legitimate (i.e., excused) absences may be just as questionable as illegitimate (i.e., unexcused) ones; therefore, the internal affairs investigator needs to maintain accurate records including, but not limited to, looking for patterns.

(2) **Alliance(s):** Not unique to police officers, people commonly associate with other people who have similar interests. Any questionable alliances are regularly addressed by policy (e.g., *Officers shall not frequent places of bad reputation, nor associate*

---

[4] (1613 – 1680) [French Classical Writer].

with persons of bad reputation). It is not the association that an internal affairs investigator focuses on, but *when the officer's position could be compromised* or, due to the officer's alliance(s), the department, other officers, or the community the officer serves could be compromised that is typically under investigation.

Years past, indirect associations in organized crime activities with rum runners, gambling rings, motorcycle clubs, the Mafia, and strong labor unions topped the list and continued into the 21st century, but now murderous drug cartels, sleeper cells, and structured street gangs could be alarming to the department.

(3) **Bribery:** A police officer accepts money in return for giving a benefit (e.g., drops a ticket) to someone. Bribes always involve at least two people and while sometimes difficult to prove, it is the investigator's responsibility to uncover any paper trail left by the officer.

(4) **Dishonesty:** Admitting one's mistake by metaphorically falling on the sword would have prevented hundreds if not thousands of police officers from losing their jobs over the years. Disturbingly, many officers are terminated from their law enforcement positions not because of what they were originally under investigation for, but for their deceptive or lying methods used to cover up what they were alleged to have done initially.

(5) **Embezzlement:** An officer who is trusted with the funds of either an organization or the budget of the police department furtively misappropriates the money from the bank account he is entrusted with to his own private account. By way of example, the treasurer of the police union writes himself checks with money from the union's account and manipulates the monthly treasurer's report to cover up the misappropriation, or the Chief of Police uses officers in the department to do construction work on his house.

(6) **Influencing:** A police officer uses his influence to secure a favor for someone in return for personal benefit (e.g., cash). The internal affairs investigator should attempt to uncover some type of financial trail whether that is cash or something material; but for the most part, influencing would be disclosed

through witness statements, undercover operations, and wire-taps. An example of influencing is when an officer accepts payment from a drug dealer in his area and in return turns a blind eye to the dealer's illegal activities. Here the officer uses his influence in being assigned to the drug dealer's area to convince him that if the dealer pays him, he has the ability to either ignore what he's doing or to keep other officers away.

(7) **Kickback:** A police officer who, for example, oversees pur-chasing, promises or awards a contract to a vendor and in return receives something for his troubles. This type of police misconduct leaves a paper trail any diligent internal affairs investigator should be able to uncover. More commonly, a kickback occurs when vendors form alliances with officers in the department to receive premature information on an upcoming contract or bid without the need to follow proce-dures like other non-connected vendors. Another form of kickback could come from a retired officer who uses an active officer to access the criminal justice information system, either for personal (e.g., suspect spouse of cheating) or professional (e.g., private investigator) reasons.

(8) **Nepotism:** Special preference (e.g., getting hired, assignments, etc.) is given to a family member based on their bloodline and not their qualifications. Through the hiring process a candidate fails the psychological exam, but because the candidate is the mayor's son the exam is either ignored or the department does psychologist shopping until one is found that will pass the son of the mayor. Then, once on the job, the mayor wants his son to be a detective and the Chief assigns him out of sequence of others more qualified. Similar to cronyism, nepotism may not be a violation, but this too would depend on the individual agency, the actions of the family member, and the special treatment in question. Again like cronyism, it is important for the internal affairs investigator to be up on the laws of the specific jurisdiction.

(9) **Cronyism:** As nepotism is the giving of special preference to family members, cronyism is the giving of special preference to friends. Unlike nepotism, which is difficult to hide from the public, many times cronyism is not discovered until a separate investigation takes place that has nothing to do with prefer-

ential treatment, or rumors start spreading around police headquarters about a suspicious relationship. Cronyism is not necessarily a violation, but this would depend on the individual agency, the actions of the "friends," and the distinctive treatment in question. It is here that the internal affairs investigator needs to clearly understand the laws of the jurisdiction before undertaking any investigation.

Things that Favor Police Misconduct

There are many intricate things that abet police misconduct, but maintaining a solid leadership base that rewards officers for doing the right thing the right way at the right time certainly limits misbehavior. Additionally, Chiefs whose careers are built on honor, honesty, and unimpeachable character serve as an example for their subordinates.

Understanding that the department has a limited amount of ranking staff members to keep track of the numerous events that occur each day, the department needs to be as transparent to the citizens they serve as the law allows. Like the first season of the FX series "Damages" perfectly demonstrates, an individual reacts to what they know; however, many times it is what the individual does not know that is important. In other words, sometimes it is not what a person wants us to know or find out that is important, but it is actually what the person did not tell or give us that will be needed to put the puzzle together. Applying this concept, openly disclosing all public records (even if published with lawful redactions) will in and of itself serve as a deterrent for police officers to cross the Rubicon. Therefore, the lack of transparency in a police department would serve as a factor that favors misconduct.

Accepting the fact that transparency can add thousands of different eyes on the inner-workings of the department and individual officers, a Chief should actively encourage, support, and embrace openness of government records created within the agency as long as their release will not put anyone in harm's way or breach an employee's rights.

Other factors that instigate police misconduct include, but are not limited to, the silencing of a public employee's free speech right; the lack of protection for whistleblowers; weak laws and accountability; and benchmarking deficiencies.

Effects of Police Misconduct

When just one police officer is accused of misconduct the outcome, even when unfounded, has an economic and social impact on the officer, department, community the officer serves, and surrounding law enforcement communities. A police officer is regarded as a consummate professional who, like no other, is empowered through an *Oath of Office* to lawfully serve and protect the innocent even if it means taking the life of another who poses a threat.

Every single allegation of misconduct must be investigated to completion; therefore, such investigations, regardless of length, always cost the taxpayers public funds (e.g., salaries, equipment, resources, etc.) that unquestionably place a financial strain on the overall budget. Maintaining the uninterrupted integrity of the department and officers reasonably will cost the taxpayers money and there's no way around it because like it or not that is the cost of doing business.

Beyond the social and economic effect, inside police headquarters officers experience a decrease in morale as they, sometimes correctly, fear they cannot do anything while on the job without being put under investigation. Undeniably, the officers are sometimes correct in their impressions, because it is sensible to recognize that a proactive officer who has greater contacts with the public will, by default, generate more complaints regardless of the officer's work ethic. In contrast, an officer with no work ethic, who answers only dispatched calls will have minimal (if any) complaints. If for no other reason, this shows the number of complaints filed against one officer versus another is of little relevance when looking at each officer's work ethic. The officer watching the grass grow probably should never have been a cop to begin with or, at the very least, should not have completed his probationary period.

Coupled with the above, as misconduct increases or is alleged, the police union's involvement also increases, causing insurmountable friction between the union and the police administration. This ongoing conflict progressively gets worse with mounting allegations and an excessive number of cases that lay dormant. As such, this often places union officials on the offensive as they strategically attack the administration and internal affairs investigators by using the media (mostly newspapers) to their advantage. (Due to confidentially concerns, the Chief is restrained from releasing the department's standpoint.) The magnification of the union's attacks can go from procedural differences, to a vote of no confidence (against the Chief), departmental charges (against the Chief and internal affairs investigators), and even criminal charges against the Chief and internal affairs investigators.

Although from an outside perspective it may appear as if the Chief and internal affairs investigators are the problem and outside intervention is necessary to bring back order to the department, the union may have strategically planned it this way to provide this false perception. Many times a vote of no confidence or threats being made against the Chief and internal affairs investigators really mean they are getting closer to uncovering something the union or their membership do not want them to find. From an internal affairs investigator's viewpoint, when the threats get stronger or start to make their way into the newspapers, it may just mean they are about to unearth the piece of evidence that will confirm the allegation under investigation.

At this point, the internal affairs investigator should reexamine the evidence gathered and the interviews conducted to make certain nothing was missed or no subsequent investigation is warranted. Regardless, all newspaper articles or news broadcasts should be gathered and maintained by the internal affairs unit and analyze them for unknown information; significant usable facts; and hidden messages.

Chapter 2
Employee Discipline in a Nutshell

At one time or another, an employer may be faced with investigating and eventually disciplining a member of their staff. While there are many aspects, both technical and legal, involved in the proper handling of employee discipline, the most critical is ensuring that the employee's discipline is based on "just cause."

These two words are probably the most important words expressed in an employee's contract or employee manual, however, are also the most widely misunderstood and ignored. "Just Cause" is defined in *Black's Law Dictionary* (6th ed. 1998) as "[l]egitimate cause; legal or lawful grounds for action; such reasons as will suffice in law to justify the action taken." *Boston Elevated Ry. Co. v. Commonwealth*, 310 Mass. 528, 39 N.E.2d 87, 112, 124. "As used in statutory sense is that which to an ordinary intelligent person is justifiable reason for doing or not doing a particular act." *Daugherty v. Admr., Bureau of Employment Services*, 21 Ohio App.3d 1, 486 N.E.2d 242, 243, 21 O.B.R. 1.

Before 1966 "just cause" was considered vague and too general by way of definition, open to the interpretation of the reviewer, and obviously difficult to implement on a practical basis. It is because of these challenges surrounding "just cause" that Arbitrator Carroll Daugherty in *Enterprise Wire Co. and Enterprise Independent Union*, 46 LA 359 (1966) established a set of concrete measurements that are still in practice today. Arbitrator Daugherty, by way of this case, created seven specific steps or standards that can and should be applied to any discharge or disciplinary matter. The first standard, question or step that needs to be answered is whether or not the rule or order implemented by the employer is reasonable. That is "was the employer's rule or managerial order reasonably related to: (a) the orderly, efficient, and safe operation of the employer's business, and (b) the performance that the employer might properly expect of the employee?" *Id*. Although management maintains a unilateral right to make rules, those rules must be reasonable in themselves and their application and are always open to the grievance procedure. However, there are five specific categories that determine whether a rule is unreasonable as opposed to reasonable. Those five categories as depicted in *Just Cause: The Seven Tests*[5] are (1) rules or orders that are inconsistent with the contract, (2) rules that conflict with an

---

[5] Koven, A., Smith, S., and Farwell, D. (1992). *Just Cause: The Seven Tests*, BNA Books, Arlington, VA (pp. 89 – 142).

established past practice, (3) rules or orders that affect employees' lives on the job that interfere with employees' personal rights, (4) rules or orders affecting employees' private lives off the job, and (5) reasonable rules unreasonably applied.

Normally, if an employee or union believes that a rule or order is unreasonable, management will immediately hear about their concerns informally by way of grievance. It is at this stage (usually step one of the grievance procedure) that if a rule or order is truly unreasonable, the employee and/or union officials can work together with management to confirm reasonableness. However, if time elapses without discussion from the employee and/or union, one would conclude that the rule or order is acceptable and reasonable as written.

The second question is whether the employee(s) received proper notice regarding the rule or order implemented by the employer. "Did the Employer give to the employee forewarning or foreknowledge of the possible consequences of the employee's disciplinary conduct" *Enterprise Wire Co.* Notice is here separated into two parts. The employer needs to notify the employee as to what performance or lack thereof will put an employee in a position of being disciplined. The employer also has to notify the employee as to what penalty will be imposed if the employee does or does not perform.

Notice should be written, posted, and signed for by each individual employee. Initialed notices are obviously best because the employee's initials leave little doubt that the rule or order was received and reviewed by the endorser. There are other forms of acceptable notices, but the one that escapes many employers as well as employees is "past practice." Past practice in its simplest terms would be the day-to-day operations of management and employees that are implied as acceptable and enjoyed by both parties for a period of time. Ironically, many employees believe past practice is most beneficial to them as opposed to management, as they mistakenly believe a majority of past practices can be not only eliminated by management (if proper steps are followed) but, more importantly, are used by management as a tool to authenticate the operations of the agency.

There are several exceptions to the notice requirement. These exceptions, by design, are excluded from the notice requirements because society as a whole believes certain acts to be unforgivable in the workplace. A few disapproved conducts by employees would be (1) insubordination, (2) neglecting one's duties, (3) dishonesty, (4) theft, (5) threats of bodily harm, and (6) sabotage. Not only is notice excluded, but the possible consequences need not be detailed either as the penalty is said to be understood.

The third question that should be addressed is whether or not the employer conducted a sufficient investigation. Basically, "[d]id the employer, before administering discipline to an employee, make an effort to discover whether the employee did in fact violate or disobey a rule or order of management?" *Id.* Here the employer is required to conduct an investigation and to ensure that only the facts are inclusive of the outcome. An employee deserves an investigation that is adequate in nature and does not just rely on circumstantial findings, inadequate proof, assumptions or hearsay. All evidence needs to be collected as well as all necessary witnesses need to be interviewed to establish proof that the employee did in fact violate or disobey an agency's rule or order.

Questions are raised at this stage as to whether or not an employee or the accused should be interviewed regarding the allegations. This is a decision that the lead investigator needs to answer and can only be decided on a case-by-case basis; however, no interview technically is required. Many investigations are absent the accused statements for the simple fact that the elements are so overwhelming that the statement may do more damage than good to the accused. However, a benefit from interviewing will provide the employer with the employee's reason behind why he or she performed in that manner and may have some bearing on the penalty. If the latter is so, then the employer should advise the accused that the investigation is complete and any statements made from this point forward (unless incriminating) will only be used toward the penalty.

Similarly, "if the employee lies in response to questions, he can be disciplined on that basis." *LaChance v. Erickson*, 522 U.S. 262, 118 S Ct 753, 139 L Ed 2d 695 (1998). An interviewed employee is obligated to be truthful at all times because "an employee who lies during an internal investigation may be discharged without violating Title VII." *Vasconcelos v. Meese*, 907 F2d 174 (CA6 1986). Hence, employees are obligated to cooperate with the employer's investigation when the investigation and questions solicited are directly, narrowly, and specifically related to the performance of one's duty. The employee has a right to be informed of the possible charges, to confront all witnesses, and in *J. Weingarten v. N.L.R.B.*, 420 U.S. 251, 88 LRRM 2689 (1975) the court held that the employee has a right to have counsel or union representation present during any questioning, if (1) the employee believes that discipline may result, (2) the employee clearly requests that a union representative be present (note the employer need not ask), and (3) that the interview purpose is to obtain information that will be considered in penalty assessment. Before questioning, management may provide the accused with a "pre-advisement" form that details that the employer (1) Orders the employee to answer the questions, (2) only asks questions that are directly, narrowly, and specifically related to the employee's duties, and (3) advises that the answers will not be used in any criminal proceedings and the employee has the right not to answer if such answers will incriminate them. *Garrity v. State of New Jersey*, 385 U.S. 493 (1967).

Follow-up to the initial investigation is favorable for all unsettled questions. The lead investigator should close all holes and answer all questions that may arise either on the side of the employer or the side of the defense. This leaves no stone unturned and eliminates doubt, which sometimes arises after the penalty has been served.

The fourth question to be answered is whether or not the employer conducted a fair investigation or to put it another way, "[w]as the Employer's investigation conducted fairly and objectively?" *Enterprise Wire Co.* This differs from question three, which required a "sufficient investigation" as opposed to a "fair investigation." A fair investigation ensures that the due process of the accused was observed and that the case's review is completed fairly and objectively. The investigator or management official who decides the penalty should not act as the prosecutor, jury, or judge and should be presented to a higher authority before any final disciplinary action is imposed.

The fifth question is "[a]t the investigation did the employer's 'judge' obtain substantial evidence or proof that the employee was guilty as charged?" *Id*. In disciplinary hearings the "Quantum of Proof" required is most commonly by the "preponderance of the evidence." This is different from the commonly known "beyond a reasonable doubt" as needed in a criminal matter.

The employer must prove three things by the preponderance of the evidence to sustain a conviction of the case at hand.

(1) The employer must prove that the charges filed are proper. This means that the employer must prove that the charge was not arbitrary and capricious, therefore making the charges clear and reasonable and that the charges were known by the employee before the imposition of any discipline;

(2) The employer must prove the case for the discipline charged and not just for a generic form of misconduct; and

(3) There must be exact elements to back up the charges. For example: If the employee is charged with insubordination, the employer must prove the employee received notice of the order, knew what consequences would follow if the order was not followed, and the employee refused to follow the order.

It should be clearly noted that circumstantial evidence that leads to only one conclusion is acceptable in a disciplinary hearing, however, the best evidence is more direct such as witness testimony, documentation, or statements from the accused.

"Has the employer applied its rules, orders, and penalties evenhandedly and without discrimination to all employees?" *Id.* Equal treatment is the sixth question that should be addressed when considering employee discipline. This question leads one immediately to Title VI of the 1964 Civil Rights Act, and in some respects rightly so; however, it focuses more on the "disparate treatment" that one employee would receive in relationship to his/her fellow employees with respect to the other five questions. Assuming all other factors involved are equal and two employees commit the same exact offense, then treatment regarding penalties should be equal. Thus, if both employees steal a bottle of Advil from the supervisor's cabinet (when they both received notice that entering the cabinet would be wrong and that the penalty for entering it would be demotion), then both parties should receive a demotion. However, if one employee receives a demotion and the other gets suspended that treatment would not be considered equal.

In agencies both large and small, there are several reasons why members would receive disparate treatment. One of the reasons is because the supervision is ineffective. Meaning supervisor "A" runs his/her shift one way while supervisor "B" runs his/her shift another. This causes confusion among the staff and when imposing a penalty against an employee, it would not be unheard of if the employee on shift "A" is treated differently than on shift "B." This type of inconsistent discipline can be easily rectified by way of uniformly enforcing all rules and orders, which would thereby satisfy the second reason that is inconsistent and non-uniformed application of rules. The third reason is that the rules are changed without proper notification or the old rules are not enforced. This also can be rectified by following the "proper notice" as discussed above.

The final question, and probably the most argumentative one, is the question of penalty. "Was the degree of discipline administered by the employer in a particular case reasonably related to (a) the seriousness of the employee's *proven* offense, and (b) the record of the employee in his/her service with the employer?" *Id.* At this stage the elements to determine penalty go beyond the question of whether the punishment should fit the crime. "It is not socially desirable that disciplinary penalties be regarded strictly as punishment for wrongdoing. Rather, the object of the penalty should be to make employees recognize their responsibilities so that they might become better workers in the future."[6]

As there are incidents that require immediate discharge, there are also incidents that should be filtered through a process called "progressive discipline." For matters involving minor infractions of the rules or orders, management should follow a chain of discipline as mention above called, "progressive discipline." This progressive discipline is normally initiated with a verbal warning for the first offense, oral reprimands for second offenses, written reprimands, suspensions or demotions for third or subsequent offenses. As stated, the main purpose of following this procession is to modify the employee's behavior and to prevent the employee from progressing so far up the chain of discipline that he or she is saved from being terminated.

In discussing immediate discharge the offense of misconduct needs to be so serious that the employment relationship will not survive even with corrective measures. These serious misconduct offenses factor in the quality of the employee's work history as well as the employee's previous discipline received including the violations charged. As discussed above and for example: lying during an employee's interview could take a less serious offense warranting a mild penalty to that of one of summary discharge. Other examples of summary discharge would include, but not be limited to, chronic absence, gross insubordination, fighting, or striking a supervisor.

In summary, there are seven steps that an employer and employee should review with regard to any disciplinary action that is forthcoming.

(1) Reasonable rule or order;

(2) Notice;

(3) Sufficient investigation;

(4) Fair investigation;

[6] The Arbitration Process in the Settlement of Labor Disputes," *Journal of the American Judicature Society*, 31 (1947) p. 58.

(5) Proof;

(6) Equal treatment; and

(7) Penalty.

Answering "no" to any one of these seven questions should heighten your awareness to the possibility that the disciplinary decision comprises one or more factors of being arbitrary, capricious, unreasonable, or discriminatory, therefore making your case seriously flawed. However, on the reverse, answering "yes" to all of the above questions would make management's case thorough, complete, and solidified. Accordingly, being honest with yourself, whether you are the employer, employee, or union will prevent unnecessary stress, expense, and litigation.

Chapter 3
Setting the Foundation

Once a citizen files a complaint or a superior observes a violation or a subordinate reports the suspected wrongdoings of his supervisor or co-worker then for all intents and purposes the procedures to enforce discipline should already be in place. These procedures include, but are not limited to, accepting allegations, assigning the investigation, investigating the allegation, determining the outcome, and if applicable, filing the appropriate charges, having a hearing if required, and establishing an appeal process.

The Chief needs to establish rules, regulations, and policies that are clear, reasonable, and appropriately complement his philosophy. These policies need to be distributed throughout the system and it should be confirmed that every employee (e.g., Officer, Dispatcher, etc.) not only receive and read the policy, but also that the employee understands the intent and point of view of the Chief.

When putting policies together, it is always best to include those affected by the policy to assist in writing the drafts. If the officers have a recognized union, its representatives also should be made part of the discussions along with at least one member from each of the department ranks (e.g., Sergeant, Lieutenant, etc.) so that input from all levels are addressed prior to adoption and implementation. Maintaining a policy steering committee that collectively drafts new policies and periodically (e.g., annually) reviews existing policies for relevance and necessary updates can only benefit the Chief, the officers, the department, and others. If the steering committee does nothing else, someone should be assigned to accurately record the historical need and basis for new policies and justification for any policy revisions. These notes will prove useful should a policy be challenged with the note taker (i.e., steering committee secretary), at minimum, be called to testify on the Chief's and steering committee's behalf. It is these rules, regulations, and policies that will be criticized most often when discipline is imposed; therefore, they should include at minimum an acceptable, reasonable, and achievable benchmark for an officer's success and the supervisor's empowerment to address minor issues immediately.

There are many ways newly created policies and procedures can be distributed among the rank and file of a police department, but ensuring that officers understand the content and context is best accomplished through the department's chain of command. Namely, just as a paramilitary organization like a police department mandates that every member of the agency follow the department's chain of command going up, the same chain of command needs to be followed going down. Taking into account the department's chain of command and emphasizing the need for all officers to understand the Chief's philosophy as it relates to the policies of the agency, the Chief should explain *in person* to only his immediate subordinate rank (e.g., Deputy Chief(s)) the purpose of the policy, how the policy should be implemented, and the possible outcomes should the policy not be followed as written and explained. This face-to-face sender-and-receiver relationship gives the Deputy Chiefs the opportunity to ask questions, receive answers, and unquestionably understand the Chief's position to avoid any misinterpretations. The Deputy Chiefs acceptance and understanding of the new policy need to be confirmed through their acknowledgment by signing an affirmation stating they understand the material presented and that they had an opportunity to ask questions.

The Statement of Understanding below offers an excellent example of a simple and user-friendly form the Department can implement to:

(1) Confirm training was done.

(2) Confirm policies were reviewed.

(3) Limit the Chief's and agency's liability.

STATEMENT OF UNDERSTANDING
This form shall be <u>handwritten</u> by the Officer; not the Instructor.

On _____ I received retraining in the below listed topics. I understand
     (Date)

the material delivered and the instructor _____
                         (Instructor's Name)

explained any questions that I may have had.

<u>Print your name here:</u> _____

Officer's Signature:

In the space below describe in <u>detail</u> the exact training (or re-training) received [include any rule, regulation, policy, or procedure number that would apply].

Keeping with the department's chain of command, the Deputy Chiefs should train their immediate subordinate rank (e.g., Majors, Captains) in the same manner they were trained and this internal training succession on the Chief's new policy should continue until all members of the police department get an opportunity to have any questions answered. Beyond the initial training, at minimum, annual reviews of all rules, regulations, and policies should take place with the officers' signature confirming the review was completed.

Broken Window Theory of Police Misconduct

Once these policies are in place, it is imperative that all suspected violations are addressed regardless of how minor the alleged infractions are perceived. Consequently, most times the methodology of how suspected violations are addressed is not as significant as the rank and file knowing infractions will not go unnoticed.

Applying Dr. James Q. Wilson and George Kelling's "Broken Window" theory to police misconduct (i.e., the unrepaired crack in an abandoned house window will ultimately invite lawlessness into the house and eventually throughout the neighborhood) to police misconduct obligates police administrators to proactively pay attention to all suspected violations, not just the serious or major ones. Considering all rules are equal and a violation of any of them could constitute a form of insubordination, it is when an individual supervisor ignores what they personally consider a minor rule violation that over time develops an irreversible mindset in his subordinates that the department views some rules as insignificant. However, when this happens then exactly where the division is between an insignificant versus a significant rule becomes blurry among the rank and file. Similar to Wilson's theory, once it is acceptable to cross the bright-line rules the infection spreads in due course plaguing the entire agency. Breaking or not following the department's rules is troubling enough; however, once that sense of entitlement takes over an officer's ability to know the difference between right and wrong, the officer has a greater probability to go from departmental violations to criminal ones (e.g., Officer in uniform goes to a restaurant while on-duty to buy dinner and restaurant manager charges officer 50% for the meal. The next day when the officer is off-duty and in plain clothes he goes back to the restaurant, orders a meal, and displays his badge to get a discount on the meal. Although the discount may be a policy violation, displaying a badge off-duty to get a benefit is a crime.). If the department proactively reinforces their "no gratuity" policy and takes aggressive action (i.e., discipline) against officers who accept discounts or freebies, it is possible this officer would have turned down the initial discount and highly probable he would not have committed a criminal offense thereafter.

There are at least two reasons why it is incumbent on the Chief to make sure all suspected violations do not go unnoticed and both are to the betterment of his agency.

The **first** reason is because of the broken window theory of police misconduct. If a police officer has the impression the administration will overlook minor violations, the officer may continue to push the envelope to see just how far he can go. An officer who keeps pushing and continues to go unchallenged by his superiors eventually will cross the line and could end up committing a serious rule infraction, violate a criminal code, or both. The crack in the officer's armor is the administration's disregard of minor rule infractions (e.g., such as being late to work, which will lead other officers to believe they can also be late without consequences). Additionally, the officer, who was initially late and went unchallenged, will believe he can be late again. (However, if the officer's first tardy is not addressed by the supervisor, the second occurrence would have to be treated as his first.) For those departments where collective bargaining exists, the rule prohibiting an officer from being late could be overridden by the unwritten past practice[7] of indirectly ignoring an officer who is late to work.

Secondly, if the Chief allows certain rules to be broken without consequences, then the rule is literally better off not being a rule at all and could actually do more harm than good. For example, an officer who commits a serious rule infraction (e.g., sleeping on duty) gets brought up on official charges, whereby the Chief believes the officer should be terminated. If the rule prohibiting an officer from sleeping on duty comes from the same policy manual as the ignored rule about being late for work, then it is certainly understandable for the defense attorney for the charged officer to question the basis behind investigating one violation but not the other. More so, if the rule against sleeping on duty is in the same rules manual as being late for work, it is common practice for the target officer's attorney to claim the officer's supervisor or internal affairs investigator failed or refused to follow the Chief's rules. In other words, the officer's supervisor or internal affairs investigators knowingly and purposefully initiated an investigation on one rule violation but not the other. Probably the most resulting damage to the Chief, his department, and the taxpayers comes from rules that are applied in a discriminatory or retaliatory manner. In today's world,

---

[7] A past practice is established when a practice is clear, consistent, and mutually acceptable.

when this goes on in a workplace, a lawsuit for discrimination and/or retaliation is sure to follow. That is, although management can apply the rules unevenly across the board with all their rank and file, the game changes when management deliberately or inadvertently employs the rules to a chosen few. Many times this uneven handling of the officers takes place between squads; whereby, the Squad "A" Sergeant is a disciplinarian who enforces the rules evenly versus the Squad "B" Sergeant who places little or no emphasis on the rules and even less on discipline. Take for example, "A" recommending discipline for a female subordinate for the same rule violation that "B" ignores when violated by a male subordinate. This disproportionate approach to discipline from one Squad Sergeant to the next is intolerable and opens the door to civil litigation.

Documenting Discipline

Generally speaking, when Supervisor "A" has low or no records of subordinate discipline when compared to supervisor "B," who has a high number of subordinate discipline, it could mean several things:

(1) Supervisor "A" does not put as much, if any, emphasis on discipline as does Supervisor "B";

(2) Supervisor "B" becomes the target of attacks by the employees and union. These attacks will generate more complaints; or

(3) Supervisor "A" is perceived more as a friend or representative than a supervisor.

All three can be a real concern for a Chief, but the most serious problem is a Chief who is in denial by falsely believing because he has no complaints or the department's investigations are low that he has no problem in the department. In these cases, more common than not, the violations and problems are there, but either the supervisors are downright ignoring them or they are addressing the violations and problems without following proper procedures.

Across the board all supervisors should be trained equally on handling discipline and the Internal Affairs process to avoid any discrepancies in its application throughout the police department. It should be known that all the rules and regulations, which are purposefully adopted and promulgated, are applicable to all members of the department. Therefore, uniformly, it should be made crystal clear to all members that discipline will be evenly applied.

However, the supervisory responsibilities are bestowed (e.g., promotion or officer-in-charge), and now the new supervisor should be immediately familiar with the department's policies, including the disciplinary process. Supervisors should be trained on identifying problematic officers and what steps should be followed to bring those officers back into the fold of the organization. These steps could be as simple as recommending in-service training needs or recommending the officer to a confidential employee assistance program.

In doing so, supervisors should be trained on the proper implementation of the department's policies and procedures and develop a reasonable understanding of how to competently address unacceptable officer behavior or misconduct. Supervisors are being paid to be supervisors and are expected to wear many different hats, because if the supervisor fails to adhere to the Chief's policies or disregards his responsibilities then it would be the supervisor who is not meeting the department's requirements or his responsibilities under his Oath.

By default, once the supervisor accepts his new role he goes from doing the job, to supervising those who now do it. Therefore, he will now be expected to prove rational and reasonable steps were taken to assist an officer and will be expected to document what steps he took to actually accomplish or resolve the issue. Supervisors, regardless of rank, should never lose sight of the fact that the goal is to provide every opportunity for the officer to succeed – **therefore, when documenting discipline, supervisors must:**

(1) Confirm the policy states what he believes it states.

(2) Confirm the policy is clear and not open for misinterpretation.

(3) Confirm the policy was acknowledged by officer.

(4) Confirm the policy was applied consistently.

Such documentation should include who was involved, when it occurred, what policy was violated, and where it occurred. Furthermore, when supervisors write reports they should do so with the assumption that discipline may be imposed and their recommendation or the final decision of the Chief will be challenged. Therefore, supervisors need to be well prepared for all possible legal challenges.

Being well prepared includes, but is not limited to, authoring a report that spells out in a clear and concise manner the supervisor's decision process. This decision process is not just the end or conclusion, but the means the supervisor utilized to get him there. In doing all this, the supervisor must be able to justify the fairness of his decision and the steps he took in reaching it.

This fairness can be based on several factors, but it certainly should start with the confirmation that the Chief as discussed clearly relayed through the chain of command his philosophy related to the policies to the targeted officer, discipline is evenly applied, and that the officer, if applicable, was given an opportunity to correct the unacceptable behavior.

Once a supervisor understands and accepts the fact that discipline is a major part of his responsibilities it will be easier for him to accept the obligation to discipline and maintain excellent records. Furthermore, the supervisor should be aware that he controls the timing of any discipline and should make certain the unfolding events are well documented in advance of any action being taken, because judges, juries, and administrative agencies expect the employer to be very well prepared when an officer facing discipline is forthcoming.

If for nothing else, excellent documentation enhances the supervisor's credibility and can be used to refresh the supervisor's memory if and when live testimony is needed. On the other hand, poorly written documentation could bring about civil litigation and departmental discipline with the supervisor as a target. To prevent poorly written reports, they should have their reports proofread by someone in their unit who lawfully is allowed to read internal affairs investigations whenever possible.

Progressive Discipline

Many departments, by way of policy and procedure, list the potential penalties an officer could receive if and when the charges are sustained. They could start with a *Statement of Understanding* and end with *termination* (see Progressive Discipline chart).

Progressive Discipline

A. Statement of Understanding
B. Verbal Warning Reduced to Writing
C. Counseling Session
D. Counseling Notice
E. Performance Notice
F. Oral Reprimand
G. Written Reprimand
H. Suspension
I. Demotion
J. Termination

Additionally (depending on the agency),

1. Restitution
2. Monetary Fine
3. Substitution Days (e.g., give up accrued days in lieu of suspension)
4. Work Additional Days/Hours (e.g., work on day off in lieu of suspension)

Whatever progressive discipline system is in place in the department, chances are the supervisors are not following it and this could be a fatal procedural flaw in an administrative case that could also put the department at risk for civil litigation. **The easiest way to know if the supervisors are complying is to separately ask each of your squad sergeants the following questions (assuming there is a policy on being late) in succession:**

(1) If an officer in your squad was ten minutes late for work; what would you do?

(2) If the same officer was ten minutes late a week later, what would you do?

(3) If the same officer was ten minutes late two weeks later, what would you do?

Each of the three questions have only one right answer; therefore, if your squad sergeants do not answer these questions exactly the same way, the Chief's red flags should be waving. It should be alarming to the

Chief if even one sergeant does not answer the same way as the others, because that sergeant failed to follow the Department's progressive disciplinary steps (i.e., policy) as previously discussed. Hence, the policy is in place and if the sergeant does not follow the policy it could realistically be viewed as a failure and/or refusal of the sergeant to follow the policies, which would be equal to or greater than a violation any target officer would have been accused of.

However, a supervisor's failure or refusal to follow the policy is probably due to compassion or because the progressive discipline policy is not suitable to the operational needs of the department. If compassion is the reason why the supervisor is not complying then discipline is the only recourse; however, if the latter is the cause, the Chief should consider amending the policy to match the practice.

To figure out the department's "practice," all members of the department who supervise at least one person should be asked the above three questions. In hypothetically applying the progressive discipline chart listed above, a *Statement of Understanding* would be the correct answer to question number one, but most supervisors when asked question number one will probably answer they in some form merely "spoke with the officer." Concluding this is the case, as your examination will show, the progressive disciplinary policy should be modified to include a step most commonly used by the supervisors in the department (e.g., "verbal counseling"), all supervisor's should be trained on this inserted step and the updated policy needs to be actively enforced for compliance. If another such commonly used step is employed, that step also should be considered and added if appropriate. Of course, another solution is to just actively enforce the current progressive disciplinary steps, but if the supervisors believed those steps were reasonable, they would have followed them already. Here the Chief's consultation with the steering committee would probably prove fruitful and advantageous to his overall mission.

The concern with having a progressive disciplinary process that is being inconsistently followed can best be shown through an example. Sergeant A speaks with a male officer who is late and Sergeant B issues a *Statement of Understanding* to a female officer who is late. The second time the male officer is late, Sergeant A has another informal chat with him and tells him for a second time to not do it again; but Sergeant B issues a "verbal warning reduced to writing" for the female officer's second offense. With the third offense, Sergeant B gives the male officer a *Statement of Understanding* when Sergeant A gives the female officer a "counseling session" that will be placed in her personnel file for six months. The obvious first question the female officer's lawyer will ask is why after two officers are late three times the male officer is not even at step one of progressive discipline, but his female client is up to a "counseling session," which is now part of her personnel file?

Now take these two fairly minor and isolated paths taken by the two different sergeants and multiply them by the total number of supervisors in the agency and the total number of violations being addressed daily by those supervisors who are not complying with the *department's* progressive disciplinary policy. Unconditionally, the role of the internal affairs investigator is charged with impartially investigating allegations of misconduct and policy violations. Taking this into consideration, the investigator needs to remain cognizant of the fact that while the received allegations may only surround one officer of the department, it is the responsibility and role of the investigator to never limit his scope; thus directly protecting and serving the best interest of the people, agency, rank, and file.

Case in point: The investigator would be negligent and performing a disservice if he limited his investigations to that of the targeted officer(s) when the possibility exists there may be other causes (as briefed above with the sergeants) behind an officer's ongoing behavior. Therefore, the internal affairs investigator needs to monitor supervisors to make certain they are all adhering to and following the progressive disciplinary system as written.

Dispositions

There are four possible dispositions that come of an investigation, and the rules should clearly define each for their members.

(1) **Sustained:** If an investigation is determined to be sustained it means at least one of the allegations investigated had enough credible evidence to show the actions of the officer were in violation of a rule, regulation, or policy of the department. Generally, a finding of sustained means formal charges will be filed and the target officer can plead guilty, not guilty, or guilty with an explanation. If guilty or guilty with an explanation, a penalty could be imposed and carried out. If not guilty an officer may be entitled to a hearing.

Example: Sergeant observes officer without his hat on while on a school crossing post. Sergeant asks officer where his hat is and the officer admits, with an apology, that he left his hat in the

Chapter 4
The Allegations

By policy, any and all allegations of police officer misconduct should be accepted by the police department. While it is preferable that the complainant reports the allegations directly to an internal affairs investigator, that is not always possible; therefore, the highest ranking sworn official on-duty should be educated on how to accept the complaint unless directed otherwise by policy.

Accepting nameless[8] complaints or complaints from minors are not frowned upon and should be handled the same way as those where the complainant is known; however, depending on the age of the minor, any follow-up interviews should be considered being taken with the permission of a guardian or parent. Additionally, complaints from other departments or elected and appointed officials from within the same jurisdiction should be received and handled solely by internal affairs except under emergency conditions where the internal affairs investigator is not available.

For nameless complaints as much information as the complainant is willing to share should be documented with a special emphasis on things like the words spoken, voice tones, and their emotional state. Although the complainant is nameless, the investigator should make an effort to persuade the complainant to come forward, but said persuasion should be without duress and if denied the attempt should be dropped.

Taking into account that details fade over time, the complainant should be provided with an avenue to swiftly provide their account of the incident as they recall it. This means that whenever the complainant makes initial contact with the department for the purpose of filing a complaint, the complaint should be accepted through whatever means the notification was made (e.g., telephone, walk-in, e-mail, etc.). As soon as possible after the initial complaint is received, an internal affairs investigator should reach out to the complainant and capture as much information as possible to confirm or deny a foundation exists to warrant further investigation. Whether or not a sworn statement from the complainant is preferred would depend on the department's policy; however, if a sworn statement is commonplace the department may discover people will be hesitant to file a complaint. Additional fallout from taking a complainant's sworn statement is the department may

---

[8] "Nameless," because even if the investigator knows who the complainant is, but he or she asks to remain anonymous, the request should be honored to the extent of what the law allows.

find that nameless complaints will outnumber those with a name attached. On the other hand, if complainants are not sworn to their statements it sends a message to officers that their Chief may not take false allegations seriously and there is little chance the department will pursue false allegations charges, which, as discussed, will lead to people accusing an innocent officer unjustifiably.

Often, at this point, the investigator can determine if the allegations are a procedural or legal misunderstanding that can be justified through a reasonable explanation. One example of a legal misunderstanding is a driver from another state that allows for left turns on red who is stopped for making a left on red in a state that prohibits it. In these type cases, once the driver is informed of the traffic law differences between the two states the case would be closed because there was no actual complaint about the officer.

It is important to be consistent by assigning a different case number and creating a separate case file for each target officer even if there is only one complainant. Having separate case numbers and files, for each officer, adds a layer of protection that doesn't breach an officer's rights or confidentiality. Separating officers from cases and files also gives the Chief, and possibly the public, the knowledge at a glance of how many complaints were received versus how many officers were involved. Taking the assignment of the case numbers one step further, allegations should be separated into two different categories: *citizen* and *supervisory* complaints. A citizen complaint comes from outside the police department, including outside agencies and the elected and appointed officials. Supervisory complaints come from within the police department from members under the Chief's command (e.g., sworn officers, dispatchers, etc.). If for no other reason, separating the two types of complaints will give the department verification as to which supervisors actively enforce the department's rules and which ones do not. Another reason, which will be explored further, is when an officer is proactively doing police work, it is understandable they would have more citizens complaints. But when both supervisory and citizen complaints are disproportionate to other officers in the department who do the same job, then this should raise some red flags.

When not a procedural or legal misunderstanding, the investigator should spend time with the complainant explaining the internal affairs investigation procedure and at the same time reassuring the complainant that allegations against members of the police department are taken seriously and addressed with due diligence. The complainant should be assured their allegations will be kept as confidential as the law allows and they will be kept abreast of the investigator's findings.

The investigator will see to it that all the evidence the complainant possess (e.g., audiotapes, voice-messages, text messages, etc.) should immediately (e.g., five calendar days) be turned over to the investigator or it will not be considered. If necessary, the internal affairs investigator should send a regular and certified letter to the complainant's address requesting any possessed evidence.

Lastly, the investigator has an obligation to inform the known complainant that should the need arise with the filing of charges their live testimony may be needed. The complainant should also be apprised of the trial procedures, but equally reassured that a majority of the cases where officers are formally charged result in an agreed-upon settlement including, but not limited to, a last chance agreement.

Timing

No other public employee is investigated and placed so intently under the microscope than law enforcement professionals. Given that police departments, compared to other branches in government, explicitly assign one of their own officers to dig into the alleged departmental and criminal wrongdoings of their members, it should not be surprising that police officers are periodically charged with violating the department's rules or committing a crime. Understanding there are hundreds of departmental policies and just as many criminal codes, even when the target officer knows he is innocent, the reporting of an allegation will have an emotional impact on the police officer. The officer will constantly review the events leading up to the allegations in his head and will bounce scenarios off his closest friends and family members. The target officer will read and reread the policies to reassure himself that the procedures were followed and will convince himself that he did nothing wrong. The target officer's appetite will diminish and, until he is cleared, he will experience sleepless nights and at times appear hollow when being spoken to. During conversations around police headquarters, the target officer may misplace or insert words and will appear concerned while at the same time outwardly denying any concerns. It is because of the target officer's emotional turmoil that investigations should be handled as swiftly as possible. Once completed, the internal affairs commander should tell the target officer immediately of its disposition. A policy should be in place that mandates all internal affairs investigations should be completed within 20 calendar days unless there are explainable circumstances that make it impossible. Explainable circumstances could be the inability to reach or interview all the witnesses in the time frame, the wait for medical records, or the investigatory interview of the target officer cannot take place because he is on vacation; unacceptable circumstances include the investigator on vacation, mismanagement, politics, or purposeful intent. Regardless of the explainable circumstances, it is not unreasonable to keep the target officer informed of the time status as long as it does not compromise the investigation. In addition to a time limit on the investigation, the policy should provide a time limit on when the Chief needs to file charges once he has sufficient information to do so.

Nonetheless, under no circumstances should the policy include a clause that dismisses the charges should the investigation not be completed within a set time limit. Although it is reasonable to put a time limit on a Chief who receives an investigation with sufficient information to file the appropriate charges, it is unreasonable to put a set time limit on an investigator when investigations frequently expand far beyond the initial allegation. If the department locks an investigator into a time frame when investigations are due or the case shall be dismissed, it may prevent an investigator from digging further, connecting some dots, or disregarding information that may point in another direction.

Chapter 5

The Internal Affairs Investigator

The internal affairs division (aka professional standards) and every officer, regardless of rank, who are assigned by the Chief to conduct internal affairs investigations, need to answer directly to the Chief.

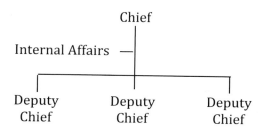

Policing the Police

It is an unfortunate fact that every single day when we pick up a newspaper we read about public officials who are accused of breaching criminal codes, Oath of Office, or their moral turpitude. These past public officials include, but were not limited to, individuals from the Executive branch (e.g., presidents, mayors, governors, cabinet members, etc.), Legislative branch (e.g., senators, assembly, House of Representative, council members, etc.), and Judicial branch (e.g., judges, court administrators, law clerks, etc.).

When a public official becomes a suspect, it is commonplace for the employer to turn to law enforcement to conduct an investigation. However, when the public official is a law enforcement officer who is suspected of violating a departmental policy or committing a crime, the police have nowhere to turn to conduct the investigation but themselves. This unique system of the police policing themselves has proven successful, but to remain successful the process must start by selecting an investigator who possesses specific impenetrable characteristics.

Furthermore, it is only the role of the investigator to investigate the allegations thoroughly, accurately, and completely; therefore, it must be done without prejudice, without any preconceived notions as to the guilt or innocence of the target officer(s), and with complete and utter impartiality. It is not the role of the investigator to assume anything or to lead any of the witnesses, including the complainant and target, into any direction because his sole mission is to be fair and balanced as his Oath of Office demands. The internal affairs investigator needs to realize, accept, and support the rationalization that he accepted this assignment based on his morals, integrity, and ethical commitments to the agency and once accepted he relinquishes any representative role for the members. The investigator also must understand he is not the member's pseudo-defense attorney and should not offer any advice legal or otherwise. The internal affairs investigator is getting paid by the taxpayers through public funds to serve as the internal affairs investigator and nothing less is acceptable.

Investigator's Characteristics

Because every law enforcement officer should be equally qualified and are held to the highest standards, it may seem oxymoronic that a Chief law enforcement officer has to consider carefully the individual characteristics before an assignment is made to the internal affairs unit. Although every police officer should possess unquestionable integrity, this quality needs to be an absolute for the internal affairs investigator. Once again: Internal Affairs investigators must possess unquestionable integrity. The investigator's integrity must be instilled and branded both on the job as well as off. Whenever possible, they should have already shown the decision makers that they will do what is right for the entity, taxpayers, and the profession as a whole regardless of the circumstances. Furthermore, the investigator needs to maintain high moral standards, a duty to the law, and an unshaken dedication to the organization's credo.

Before accepting such a crucial assignment, the investigator also has to understand and genuinely believe their Oath outweighs all other allegiances. In other words, an officer, regardless of rank, who is assigned to investigate police misconduct, needs to internally concede they are responsible to their Oath and are not acting as an Officer's Union Representative, friend or equal. This state of mind, while difficult when faced with fraternal pressures, is not impossible and the investigator needs to recognize, then overcome, any apprehensions. Before accepting this assignment, the investigator needs to clearly comprehend that at any time he could be assigned to investigate the wrongdoings of an officer who was his former police academy partner, co-worker, or his son's Godfather. Thus, maintaining professionalism even when faced with uncomfortable assignments or indirect conflicts is paramount.

Factually, internal affairs investigators are continually given un-comfortable assignments that are seen as unpopular among their brethren; therefore, investigators must be ready, willing, and able to accept the consequences that come with the assignment. Those disturbing consequences include, but are not limited to, being called names (e.g., rat, cheese eater, etc.); becoming the target of attacks by union officials; attempted expulsion from the union; and family members being retaliated against.

Furthermore, like many assignments in law enforcement, the investigator will need to work extended hours, holidays, weekends, nights, and many times responsibilities will be in direct conflict with the investigator's personal life. Considering these assignments are sometimes demanding, it is important for the chief law enforcement officer to assign an officer who is proactive and self-motivated with an ability to communicate respectfully with elected and appointed officials as well as the community leaders, business owners, residents, and all concerned persons.

Although to unsworn individuals the above considerations may not seem significant, when assigning an officer to the internal affairs unit, the right selection is essential as it relates to the thin blue line.

Thin Blue Line

For no other reason than the job, recruits and rookie police officers commonly find their unsworn friends slowly distancing themselves from their relationship and their newly found sworn peers growing closer. As the civilian friendships progressively disappear and the cop solidarity gradually gets stronger, the thin blue line metaphorically becomes threaded through a police officer's soul. This devoted bond intriguingly has more to do with the blue uniform than the person wearing it or the patch on the officer's shoulder. Benevolently, it does not matter if the officer is from New Jersey, California, Montana or South Carolina; the embedded unity based on the uniform is real.

Therefore, unlike investigating the wrongdoings of a mayor or borough clerk, when an internal affairs investigator, who wears a blue uniform, receives an allegation involving another officer who also wears a blue uniform the methodology in accepting, initiating, and investigating the complaint needs to be strategically calculated. Namely, when a police officer investigates, for example, the mayor of a municipality, he does not need to first separate himself from the described hardened camaraderie built at a time when his civilian friends were replaced with the blue line. That's why, first and foremost, the investigator needs to emotionally accept his need to separate himself from his role as an internal affairs investigator from that of a sworn member of a very close-knit group that maintains a powerful union across the planet.

Union Representative

Considering the thin blue line exists and could have an influence on the internal affairs investigator it is important for the Chief Law Enforcement Officer not to assign an officer to the internal affairs unit who actively serves as a representative of the union (e.g., President, Vice-President, Delegate, Treasurer, etc.), has the potential of serving as a representative (e.g., candidate in upcoming election), or an officer who comes across more distant from the mission and philosophy of the organization than the union's constitution and by-laws.

Allowing an officer to be assigned to internal affairs when a possible conflict exists not only causes concern for the investigator and the department, but could be disadvantageous to the outcome of the investigation, the Union and the members, and the confidence from the community.

Three additional positions the internal affairs investigator should not be in while actively assigned to the unit are the union's grievance committee, a mediator for grievances, and the collective bargaining team. Although the latter is not as crucial to avoid as the other two, there are many times when collective negotiations result in external agencies' involvement and an internal affairs investigator needs to remain impartial at all times. Obviously, any connection to the grievance procedure should be avoided by the investigator, because it is more than likely the grievant will use the grievance procedure to defend his actions by attacking the steps taken by the internal affairs investigator.

Over the years there have been some very sharp, well educated, and dedicated union representatives who unquestionably had sharper pencils than their internal affairs investigator adversaries. Even today there are union presidents, vice-presidents, and delegates who are far more advanced in the practices, procedures, and the rights of an officer; however, with the various in-service internal affairs educational opportunities available now and the huge networking base available, this once unbalanced scale has since become much more balanced. Remarkably, chief's are finally understanding the need for competent and well-trained internal affairs investigators; thus, finding once weak or non-existent policies and no investigators, we now see across the country effective and efficient policies and devoted internal affairs investigators. One difference that has changed over the years is that target officers are not asking their union's representatives for help when they are under investigation, but instead they are going directly to an attorney. This seems to be a common practice now, but over the years this only happened when the union believed the internal affairs investigator was sharper than their own representatives. Regardless of the reason, lawyers are used more often now and that alone is a good sign for how internal affairs, professional standards, and the investigator have grown over the years.

Interestingly, three decades ago even labor attorneys were not as well versed in the practices of police misconduct as they are today. However, with the thousands of court opinions now on this topic across the country and the millions of dollars the law firms are making off of cases involving police discipline, today there are firms that dedicate their entire practice to just defending police officers. Firms that went from one attorney doing contract law to ten attorneys handling police misconduct or sole practitioners with upwards of 500 police officer clients a year. Beyond the arbitrary calls these law firms receive from target officers, some police unions make available to their members an inexpensive insurance protection plan that covers the costs of attorneys and experts for a target officer under administrative and criminal investigations.

To counter politics, retaliation, whistle-blowers' vengeance, unscrupulous supervisors, and intentional rights violations, a protection plan is worth every single penny; however, when the plan is used to do nothing more than delay the implementation of deserved penalties from being carried out or is used by officers who have illegitimately crossed the Rubicon from being removed, then the system is plagued with some serious flaws that need to be corrected. When the taxpayers have to spend sometimes hundreds of thousands of dollars to remove a rogue cop that even the union and their membership believe is unfit to be on the job, the protection plans do more harm than good and are in need of a serious overhaul.

Sharpening-the-Pencil

To be a good internal affairs investigator it will require a substantial amount of reading, writing, memorization, and listening. While these qualities can be broadened after an officer is assigned to the unit, it is best to select someone who displays an interest in the first two (i.e., reading and writing) and the ability to fine tune the remaining two (i.e., memorization and listening). Internal affairs investigators are responsible for knowing the rules, regulations, policies, and procedures as well as how they apply to all different sets of circumstances. Furthermore, an investigator needs to be intimately familiar with the Personnel Manual(s), all union contracts including, but not limited to, union members' rights, management rights, and each and every section within the contracts that eventually affect an officer who becomes a target of an investigation.

Besides the numerous documents listed already, an internal affairs investigator also has to be familiar with the federal and state statutes, relevant case law, and any codes in effect in the target officer's jurisdiction. While initially many officers believe the relevance of officer rights like Garrity and Weingarten are straightforward, once they are assigned to internal affairs and obligated to protect the target officer's rights, they swiftly discover the multifaceted aspects of each.

Even with all the knowledge retained through the written publications and their understanding of the proper application, an investigator is not an investigator unless he is capable of networking with other internal affairs investigators.

Networking

Although being well-informed makes for a good internal affairs investigator, to be a great internal affairs investigator he needs the personality and unfettered ability to network with other investigators not only in their surrounding area, but across the county, state, and at times the country.

While some states, like New Jersey and North Carolina, have statewide internal affairs groups (e.g., *New Jersey Internal Affairs Association:* www.NJIAA.com and *North Carolina Internal Affairs Investigator's Association:* www.NCIAIA.org), there is also a national group, *National Internal Affairs Investigator's Association* (http://niaia.us/index.php), investigators can join; however, at minimum, if they do nothing more than associate themselves with other investigators bordering their jurisdictions it is better than nothing.

Being academically aware of the laws and procedures to conduct a thorough, accurate, and complete investigation of an individual who wears a blue uniform is important, but being able to communicate directly with others who may have conducted *similar* (i.e., the fact patterns for these investigations are never exact) investigations is essential. An example of this can be found in this book where there are pages filled with valuable information on how to investigate police misconduct. But in many investigations it is what is not in this book that an investigator will need to learn for the trials and tribulations the investigator will face head-on, but what other internal affairs investigators have experienced or successfully and unsuccessfully practiced.

Training

Realistically, it is impossible to know all there is about investigating police misconduct, but at minimum a new investigator should take a basic course by someone who has experience in conducting these types of investigation. Supplemental training should also be strongly considered with respect to interviewing techniques, identifying deceptive behavior, Garrity and Weingaren Rights, and employee discipline to mention a few. After these basic courses are completed, the seasoned investigator should begin to focus on more detailed courses that center on topics like incapacity, police officer involved domestic violence, controlling absenteeism, workplace privacy, free speech, and so on.

Unquestionably, without actually conducting an internal affairs investigation, possessing a wealth of information that comes from a book or through a classroom setting will be most effective once the principles learned are actually tried; therefore, mentorship from a seasoned internal affairs investigator is highly recommended.

"Business Is Business" and FORGET Compassion

While the mechanics of an investigation are explored within, investigators need to recognize and conclusively accept that their role as an internal affairs investigator is limited to collecting evidence, conducting interviews, and thoroughly putting together the conclusions uncovered with no preconceived notion as to the results or the disposition (e.g., sustained or non-sustained). Irrefutably, every investigator is charged with conducting an investigation without injecting compassion or inserting their personal prejudices; hence, business is business. The need for treating every investigation with a business approach is vital. A "business-is-business" approach is important considering that each officer under investigation and every single piece of evidence collected or information obtained is distinctly unique and warrants a methodology that throughout the investigation remains impartial and unbiased.

When the target officer holds membership in an influential brotherhood, to conscientiously suppress compassion during an investigation is easier said than done; however, without a shred of doubt, any compassion inserted will serve as the investigator's Achilles' heel. It is weakness the target officer's defense attorney will strategically use against the investigator should the opportunity arise. A typical example of this is when the defense attorney, after the charges are lodged, discovers the investigator failed to follow an established step or procedure either intentionally or unintentionally and he demands the Chief open an investigation into his insubordination to the Chief's policy. (Complaints filed against the internal affairs investigator are becoming more frequent and many times it is the investigator's compassion that will be the underlining basis behind the charges.)

Chapter 6
The Target Officer

Incompetence

Just as deadly error number five (i.e., relaxing too soon) for law enforcement personnel serves as the axis to all other deadly errors, competence is the nucleus that controls one's ability to function properly in society. As authors Peter and Hull point out in *The Peter Principle*, "Occupational incompetence is everywhere. Have you noticed it? Probably we all have noticed it."[9] *Merriam-Webster Online Dictionary* defines incompetence as "unable to function properly."[10] This dysfunction is all too familiar. For example, when was the last time you drove away from a fast food restaurant and your order was incorrect; read about an instrument left in a patient after leaving the operating room; or asked a police officer for directions only to get misguided further?

Unfortunately employee incompetence, as described above, happens every second of every minute of every day. This is confirmed by the number of employment and customer lawsuits settled, either through trial or consent, in the United States annually. In 2001 alone, there were over 11,000 tort cases filed with a median punitive damage award of $50,000.[11] Law enforcement leaders have seen a significant rise in lawsuits pertaining to a police department's failure to train, failure to supervise, negligent hiring, and negligent promotion.

In society, through every facet of life, the public is left dealing with employees on a daily basis in their positions but cannot handle the responsibility. As alluded to above, law enforcement, unfortunately, is not excluded from this tarnished characteristic and in some agencies it begins with the hiring and promotional procedures. Procedures that are flawed by one or several factors including, but not limited to, political patronage, legislation, past practice, and favoritism. This imperfect design gives the leaders the ability to look right through, ignore, or entertain the incompetence at every level of law enforcement from the newly hired officer on probation all the way up to the Chief law enforcement official.

---

[9] Hull, Raymond & Peter, Laurence J. (1969). *The Peter Principle.* Cutchogue, New York: Buccaneer (p. 20).

[10] http://www.m-w.com/cgi-bin/dictionary/book=Dictionary&va=incompetent

[11] http://www.ojp.usdoj.gov/bjs/civil.htm

This ignorance is tolerated, in most agencies, until the delusional observers can no longer keep hidden the escalated disruption caused by the employees outward incompetence. This cycle, in law enforcement, begins with the probationary police officer who lands the job because he has an impressive resume, is politically connected, passes the right tests or is the *best of the worst* of all submitted applicants.

In explaining my *best of the worst* theory, I offer the following example:

When a police agency announces 10 new hiring openings, the agency will receive, for example, 100 applications to fill those 10 positions. In other words, out of those 100 applicants, 90 of them will not get hired, but 10 will. However, in reality, the 10 applicants left may still not be the best candidates for the agency, but the chief has limited options:

- *Hire the ten best out of the 100.*

- *Don't hire anyone and remain understaffed.*

- *Don't hire anyone and start the hiring process all over again.*

The cost of the hiring process generally prohibits options two and three; therefore, in reality, the Chief could end up hiring those 10 applicants who in retrospect were only the best of the worst. Now to clarify this theory's principle, it obviously is not always the case where those hired are the best of the worst, but the point behind the principle is that the Chief can only choose from those who apply and knowing this going in raises the possibility that all 100 that applied are not properly suited for the hiring agency. Under those circumstances, no hiring should take place and the hiring process should start all over again until the properly fitted applicants walk through the door.

Once sworn in, it is usually obvious the newly hired rookie is unready, unwilling, or unable to perform adequately; however, field training officers, partners, and supervisors consistently ignore or turn a blind eye to the fact that he cannot function competently. Nevertheless, for a variety of reasons, including their own incompetence, those governed with the responsibility to react, fail to let the rookie go.

After probation this same officer, possibly for the same reasons as to why he was hired in the first place, moves through the ranks mismanaging, disorganizing, and disrupting the agency; conceivably, hiring someone in his own image. This scenario could easily have been prevented by simply removing the probationary officer once his incompetence was known to be incurable, but that's not always the case.

A majority of the time an employee's competent in one position, but his level of incompetence does not expose itself until he is promoted or assigned different responsibilities. More so, in law enforcement, being promoted in-and-of-itself is what permits the ability to be promoted again (e.g., in most agencies, to be considered for the rank of Chief, one must first be a Deputy Chief, Captain or Lieutenant).[12] Time and time again, officers are promoted to a higher level of authority, and it is there they openly display their incompetence when conducting the responsibilities they're assigned. Here, probation is minimal if at all; therefore, by the time their incompetence is disclosed, "just cause" (as discussed in chapter 2) is needed to terminate. "Cause" that most supervisors are not documenting, not willing to address, or once again are too incompetent themselves to recognize. Systemically, the problem exists in every aspect of one's life; however, when it exists in law enforcement it builds a subculture from within that in due course can lead to abuse, dishonesty, corruption, and the like.

An officer's eventual date with internal affairs is predictable if and when the incompetent officer goes unfettered from probationary to regular officer or a competent officer gets promoted or is prematurely reassigned to a position they are too incompetent to handle.

Sorry, You Didn't Make Probation

Categorically, there's a difference between having a valid reason for letting a probationary police officer go versus sharing those reasons with the officer personally. The fact of the matter is, a reason is needed before letting an officer go, but if the department documented and discussed the concerns throughout the officer's tenure, there's usually no need to provide the probationary officer with those reasons.

Before you ponder whether or not the officer should be let go, review the officer's file and ask yourself: What facts do I possess that lead me to conclude the officer did not make probation and should be let go? If the answer is "nothing," it would be difficult to justify this officer's departure during a hearing before an impartial Judge. On the other hand, if the probationary officer's personnel file contains consistently negative employee evaluations, descriptive supervisor notes, and evidence the probationary officer is not competent enough

---

[12] Generally, patrol officers are not eligible for the Chief's position.

to serve in the police department, the agency should have firm grounds to defend the actions of the decision makers. The answer to this will be apparent as the Chief prepares his presentation to anyone of authority should the need arise.

Obviously, if no rational reason or supportive documents exist that point to the logical conclusion behind the officer's discontinuance, someone from a higher authority may eventually ask why the Chief would let an officer go who has an unblemished record. For that reason, the Chief should not only encourage the field training officer and supervisors to document their experiences—both positive and negative—with the officer, but also the exact discipline (i.e., training) and results the officer received throughout his time with the department. In most cases, if properly done, the officer understands and internally accepts his fate long before the formal notification is made to him that he did not make probation. The Chief understandably is under no obligation to inform the officer as to the detailed collective reasons why this decision is being carried out. However, if not properly done, when an officer does not receive the reason(s) it is highly probable he will seek the assistance of an attorney who may allege the reason(s) are anything but just.

Unquestionably, as unpleasant as it is to let go a probationary officer who didn't make probation, it is more unpleasant to keep an incompetent officer in the department for years. Furthermore, do not wait until the twelfth month if it is evident from the record that this officer is not acting in accordance with the philosophy of the Chief, department, or public policy. Along these lines, swift personnel movement should be taken once it's determined this officer's continued employment with the organization is not in the best interest of all parties involved.

Prevention

Regrettably, there's no absolute solution to eliminating incompetence in law enforcement; however, implementing at least one realistic step can make it closer to reality. That step is through in-service education and training; however, with staffing and funding being so scarce police administrators cannot offer the training some officers want or need.

Moreover, police departments, although separated only by an imaginary border, place a different emphasis on education. Some departments pay for college, while others don't; some agencies allow their officers to attend class during their work week or offer to those officers who are attending class an opportunity to do homework when on-duty, while others won't. Furthermore, some officers have a majority of their college paid for in advance [by the taxpayers] and receive incentives for earning college credits or a college degree, but others don't.

By limiting one's workplace incompetence, at minimum, society will witness a reduction in very expensive litigation. Litigation that could have certainly been reduced by taking the average punitive damages paid out annually and supplement the police department budget with this amount to be earmarked solely for educating those who wear a blue uniform. Unfortunately in many cases either the departments are not offering incentives or when they do the officers fail to take advantage of those benefits offered.

Chapter 7

The Interview

Whether you use official written questionnaires (aka: "White Sheets"—see Appendix A) or interview using audio or video equipment, the method used should remain consistent. Consistency means the use of one method for every single witness, all targets, and on all cases unless there's a rational explanation (e.g., witness is stationed overseas and a conference audio of the interview is more appropriate than the use of video) to justify a switch.

Regardless of the method used to record live statements, it is important to immediately transcribe the statements and review them as soon as possible. More times than not, the investigator records the target officer during the interview, but to either save the agency money or because the investigator believes he won't need it, the investigator fails to get the interview transcribed. The decision to not transcribe could, and more than likely will, result in crucial information going unnoticed.

As beneficial as gaffes, non-verbal communication, and questions are to internal affairs investigations, the exact words spoken are invaluable. It is the capturing of the target's words in his own hand-writing to later quote verbatim in the reports and/or emphasize during a trial that has had many departments switch from audio recording interviews to using "White Sheets."

The use of White Sheets was initiated on or about 1996, whereby, the target officer, instead of a face-to-face investigatory interview, is served with the questions he would have been asked if an in-person interview took place.

In creating the White Sheet method of interviewing the target officer, the following is successfully accomplished:

- Waters down the adversarial relationship among the internal affairs investigator, target officer, and union representative that typically exists during the traditional face-to-face interview.

- Eliminates all *Weingarten* rights issues. The target officer after being handed the Administrative Investigation Only Form receives the White Sheets and has the ability to speak with his attorney, parents, union representatives, and whoever he feels comfortable with prior to answering the questions and returning the White Sheets to internal affairs.

- Removes the need to transcribe statements, because the target officer answers the questions in his own handwriting. Additionally, there will be no inaudible statements.

- Gives the investigator the unfettered ability to analyze the target officer's written words, examine the content and context, and proficiently apply statement analysis to uncover obvious deceptiveness.

Marital Privilege

Marital privilege, in a nutshell, protects all communications between a married couple in civil and criminal cases. Therefore, if an investigation necessitates an interview of a spouse with regards to any private communications they may have had, more likely than not, the request will be challenged successfully. Additionally, it is highly probable this communication will also be excluded if the married couple is in the same department and the communications took place while they were on-duty at the same time.

Alternatively, there are times when a spouse is a witness to an incident and their communications are immaterial for the allegation under investigation. Under those circumstances (e.g., cop husband is driven home by non-cop wife, but allegation the following day from a third party is that cop husband drove drunk from the bar), when the spouse possesses information void of any private communications and the spouse volunteers a statement, the statement should be taken. However, even under the circumstances where their private communications are of no significance, if the spouse is unwilling to offer a statement, the chances of obtaining one are unlikely.

Off-duty Conduct

Questions being presented to an officer must be specifically, directly, and narrowly related to the officer's role and responsibilities. The challenge on what is or is not specifically, directly, and narrowly related is highly probable when the allegations under investigation take place off-duty; therefore, the Chief needs to establish a clearly written, understood, and accepted policy on what conduct off-duty is unacceptable. Despite management's perspective on what is unacceptable, unless prohibited by statute, regulation, or case law, restrictions on off-duty conduct are a subject that is permissibly negotiable.

As one court opined, "when an employee's private life is the center of rumors, when it adversely affects his fellow workers, when it corrupts his family members, and when it results in complaints to his employer, governmental intervention is warranted," *Fabio v. Civil Service Commission of the City of Philadelphia*, 489 Pa. 309, 325 A.2d 82 (1980); this formed an ambiguous base-line regarding off-duty conduct, but what remains unsettled will be the application of any policy, the interpretation of the base-line, and the discipline that comes from both. Disappointedly, but certainly understandably, there are no bright-line rules or tests that a Chief can copy and paste to form a model policy. However, **there are a few points and/or questions the Chief could first look at before deciding whether an investigation should even be considered.**

People or Cop

Officers are "people" first and cops second. Actually, the only reason the cops are cops is because they are people. The people referred to here are the ones referred to in the United States Constitution; specifically, in part, "We the *People* of the United States" (emphasis added).

When an investigator receives an allegation about an officer in the agency, the investigator should separate the people from the cop (or vice versa) and see if after the division "We the People" outweighs the cop. If so, need there be any more written here?

The Link

What precisely (yes, "precisely") linked the officer to the police department (e.g., officer in uniform, flash his badge, known D.A.R.E. officer by complainant, announce his rank or department, etc.)? While a direct link (e.g., in uniform) to the police department normally will hold more weight than an indirect link (e.g., uninvolved patron believes individual is a police officer) neither can be discounted completely, but with a sustained finding the penalty could be lessened with the latter.

Action / Inaction

In detail, what exactly did the officer do or not do that called him to the attention of others? In other words, did his actions or inactions go against, with unquestionable certainty, an established written policy, statute, or public policy that he knew or should have known about beforehand? On the other hand, did he do what any other reasonable and prudent "people" would have done in exactly the same situation and the only reason a complaint is filed is because he wears a blue uniform?

Touch
How exactly did the officer's touch reflect on the police depart- ment? Did the tentacles of the officer's off-duty conduct have a direct or indirect affect on the police department and what actual affect did the touch have?

Specifically, Directly, and Narrowly
Stop and think about the questions the target officer will be asked surrounding this investigation to confirm those presented will be *specifically*, *directly*, and *narrowly* related to the target officer's role and responsibility as a law enforcement officer. Like all internal affairs investigations, the questions should not serve as a fishing expedition to build a case against the officer; therefore, knowing even a summary of the allegations should provide ample informa- tion to draft questions to know if they are or are not going to be intimately related to the officer's job.

However, once the policy is established or the Chief assigns the case, it is only the internal affairs division investigator's responsibility to look into allegations of noncompliance. In doing so, the investigator takes no position as to, for example, the constitutionality of the policy, but examines whether or not the negotiated policy was violated based on the evidence gathered, witnesses interviewed, and the investigatory interview with the target officer.

In taking on this position, the internal affairs investigator will be placed in uncomfortable positions; whereby, the target officer will eventually be interviewed as it relates to a departmental investigation. Understanding this, the department should assist the investigator by having a clear-cut policy that tells verbatim what is expected of the officer when he is the target in an administrative investigation. For example, the policy should make it clear that the target officer has an obligation to be cooperative with the investigator and is required to answer questions that are specifically, directly, and narrowly related to his law enforcement position. The policy should point out that this obligation to cooperate also extends to current investigations con- ducted by outside agencies. The policy should clarify the target officer's administrative rights and refer the target to any negotiated benefits as expressed and agreed upon through the collective bargaining process; however, the policy should not spell out the officer's benefits listed in the bargaining agreement, because if duplicated in the policy they are technically no longer subjects of bargaining and if unilaterally modified the union may challenge the amendment based on an past practice. Additionally, the target should be made aware that supplemental or special reports may be required, and that the target has no justified right to refuse to answer questions or provide a special report just because the responses given will conclusively prove the target officer's guilt.

The reasons behind why a target officer takes steps to intentionally and deliberately delay the investigatory interview is not so perplexing:

- If they delay long enough it may be forgotten about.

- Complainant will lose interest in pursuing.

- Something else bigger will come along and redirect the investigator's attention.

- They can use "I don't recall" more frequently.

- Evidence will disappear.

- Gives target more time to think through the incident, etc.

Predictably, if not for the target officer looking for ways to postpone the interview, it is highly probable that more officers under administrative investigation would forgo the use of a representative during administrative questioning all together.

However, considering that is not the case, the internal affairs investigator should notify the target officer in writing that an investigatory interview will take place on a specific date and time. Notice of the interview should be provided to the target with ample time to give the officer an opportunity to make arrangements with a representative if he so chooses. Frequently and more times than probably is reasonably justified, the target officer in attempting to delay the interview claims either a representative or the specific representative he wants to use is not available on the scheduled date or time and seeks a postponement. Although some investigators find it unreasonable, uncalled for, and extreme to wait until the target officer's specific representative is available, allowing the target a representative he feels comfortable with during the investigatory interview is a very small allowance. More so, depending on the size of the police union, not every union representative is familiar with Garrity, Weingarten, or the internal affairs process, and by refusing a reasonable accommodation the target officer may argue their forced representation was un-satisfactory. (Granted while such an argument sounds ridiculous, it does not mean it will not be presented by the target's attorney.) Besides the union's representative, if the target officer requests an unusual third person to act as his representative—again while some investi-gators feel it extreme, in most cases where the person will not disrupt the interview—the request should be honored.

Regardless of the reason behind the target officer's request(s) for a delay, the investigator should have the target officer document the exact reason for the request. (The reason may be untruthful, warranting a collateral investigation.) Once received, the investigator should honor the request, especially if it is a first-time request. However, instead of simply granting an extension, the investigator should provide the target with a scheduling window (e.g., Monday 12 p.m.; Tuesday 9 a.m. or 1 p.m.) and have him provide the date and time from the provided window.

Tape Recording

The limited states with two-party notification laws aside, the remaining states with one-party notification laws should not assume the investigatory interview is not being audio taped by the repre-sentative. The representative, not the target officer, will more than likely be the holder of the audio-recorder, because in most agencies where the states authorize one-party notifications a policy is in effect prohibiting members from tape recording without the Chief's written consent. To insure surreptitious recordings did not take place by the representative, the investigator should place the target officer on notice that secret recordings are discouraged (maybe even prohibited), but if the target knows or should have known about any recordings, he is to provide an identical copy immediately.

With regards to the investigator tape-recording the investigatory interview, this decision needs to be determined either by policy or through the union's collective bargaining agreement. The internal affairs investigator should not be left to his discretion on a case-by-case basis as to whether he should tape the interview or not. This means if there is no policy and the collective bargaining agreement does not dictate one way or the other as to the taping of interviews, the Chief needs to make certain this is done. If taping is done, all parties should obviously and unquestionably be notified beforehand; if charges are filed, a copy of the recording should be provided to the target.

In *Newark Bd. of Ed.*, P.E.R.C. No. 83-156, 9 NJPER 368, 369 (14167 1983), the Commission found that "established labor relations law does not permit one party to impose [a tape recording] precondition on the processing of grievances." The Commission relied on the following cases in support of its conclusion: *Morton-Norwich Products, Inc.*, 94 LRRM 1696 (1977) (union violates federal Labor/Management Relations Act when it insists on tape-recording grievance proceedings in absence of contractual provision or past practice allowing tape-recording); *City of Reading*, 12 PPER 180 (12182 1981)(PLRB holds that employer cannot insist upon tape-recording grievance sessions); and, *Bartlett-Collins Co.*, 99 LRRM 1034 (1978), *aff'd* 639 F.2d 652, 106 LRRM 2272 (10th Cir. 1981) (tape-recording negotiations session is not a mandatorily negotiable subject).

On a parallel note, videotaping would be treated the same because the purpose of videotaping is being done not only to record visual but the audio as well.

In the Room

The room, to be specific, should be a location chosen by the internal affairs investigator and the time should be in the best interest of the case, investigator, target officer, and agency. The investigatory interview should be conducted with the utmost professionalism and this includes reasonable breaks for food or personal needs. Once complete, but before the target is sworn to his statement, the investigator should spend a few moments reviewing the target's statement and supplemental information provided. If nothing else, the review will put aside any misunderstandings the target may attempt to raise at a future date.

Lastly

The most important thing to remember about interviewing, whether it is done through White Sheets, audio taping, or some other method, is to conduct an investigatory interview on the target officer even if the preponderance of all credible evidence points to the target's guilt. **Even if not needed to collaborate what the investigator already knows, the investigatory interview will:**

(1) Lock the target officer into his reasoning(s) (e.g., defense).

(2) Prevent a showy explanation after discovery is released.

(3) Uncover any dishonesty.

Chapter 8
The Jacket

An internal affairs investigator's primary responsibility is to impartially interview all interested parties, gather relevant facts, and address collateral issues without delay. Once the investigator completes a thorough investigation he then needs to write a report.

The purpose of the report, like all police reports, is to provide the reader with a neutral narration of all the details assembled in a logical, user-friendly format that draws conclusions with respect to the suspected violation's disposition.

A typical format should have no less than five sections: Facts, Violations, Summary, Findings, and Recommendations.

(1) **Facts**

This section includes, but is not limited to, the events in chronological order that took place up to the event being investigated.

A. The reason the events are listed in chronological order is because when an investigator testifies in a hearing the case is generally presented in that sequence; therefore, if the facts are recorded in order it will be easier at trial.

B. Listing each fact using bullet points is easier than paragraphs for instances when the investigator needs to refresh his memory and it also keeps events, dates, and times stamped.

(2) **Violations**

This section includes, but is not limited to, all the ordinances, rules, regulations, orders, directives, and procedural violations that the target officer violated.

A. While the order of the violations is of no significance for each individual case, consistency from one case to the next will be helpful; therefore, it is recommended to list the most serious violation first and in descending order after that.

B. The exact definition of the violation should accompany the violation number. Doing this keeps everything related to this investigation in one document to avoid the need for numerous different documents while testifying.

(3) **Summary**

This section includes, but is not limited to, a comprehensive summary of the events correlating the facts as bulleted in section #1 to the violations listed in section #2.

A. The summary, unlike the facts, should be written in a paragraph easy-to-follow layout.

(4) **Findings**

This section includes, but is not limited to, the investigator's findings (Sustained, non-Sustained, Exonerated, Unfounded) and reasons why.

A. When the investigator is documenting why a specific rule, etc., is sustained, it should be made clear in this section that the reasons presented are not inclusive, but only summarize the investigator's underlining basis behind his conclusions.

B. Policy flaws, as uncovered through this specific investigation, should be recorded in this section.

C. What should not be in this section, but in an entirely separate investigation report, is collateral findings involving other officers. (Other officers' information is confidential and including it in this report could be a violation of other officers' rights.)

(5) **Recommendations**

This section includes, but is not limited to, the investigator's recommendation about what the penalty he believes should be imposed, because nobody, including the Chief, will have such an intimate insight as to what happened. It is the investigator who absorbed and dissected every word spoken or written and observed the non-verbal communications; therefore, it is the investigator who should offer his recommendations with respect to a fair and reasonable penalty. (The Chief does not need to accept the investigator's recommendation.)

Internal Affairs Files

The internal affairs commander, as noted, directly answers to the chief of police and should be the central depository of all internal affairs records as well as all individual officer discipline. To be exact and to avoid risk, individual supervisors should not maintain separate files on those under their command. For confidentiality purposes, there should be only one internal affairs file on each officer in the department and these files should be accessed under very limited circumstances.

Besides the jacket, the internal affairs commander should keep track of past, current, and future investigations through an index type quick reference system that categorizes, at minimum, the case number; date, officer's name; officer's badge number; most serious allegation; complainant's last name; lead investigator; and resulting disposition. While many departments use an index card filing system or an electronic spreadsheet (see below) there are several professional software programs on the market a commander could use that ultimately does the same thing the index card or spreadsheet classification system accomplishes.

Case Number	Date	Officer's Last Name	Officer's Badge No.	Most Serious Allegation	Complainant's Last Name	Lead Investigator	Disposition
IA2010-1	1-Jan-10	Patrick	115	Insubordination	Star	Verry	Sustained

The internal affairs jacket should include every single record associated with the investigation and immediately after the record becomes a part of the jacket, the record shall be considered confidential. Including the initial complaint, the investigator should pack the jacket with all tape recordings, including telephonic voice-messages and interviews; written statements; field notes (if applicable); chain of custody forms; use-of-force reports; pictures; phone records; videotapes; initial reports and all supplemental reports; transcripts; attorney correspondences; and so on.

Confidentiality

As stated, the internal affairs files and all items in the file should be treated as confidential. Only under very limited circumstances are these files permitted to be released and for the most part those receiving a file are required to preserve the integrity of the material within.

The four limited reasons an internal affairs file may be released are:

(1) **Formal Charges**
   If charges are filed against the target officer and the officer, after pleading not guilty, requests a hearing on the charges, he

would be entitled to a copy of the pieces of the jacket that led to the charges. Under these circumstances, the target officer and his attorney would need the file to prepare for and present their defense in opposition to the department's position.

A. It is not the actions and/or inactions of the target officer that the target officer's defense attorney defends against, but it is the department and/or the investigator's failure to follow the policies while conducting the investigation.

B. Even when the target officer's lawyer realizes his client's actions and/or inactions are indefensible, frequently the only challenge left is linked to the severity of the penalty. For example, if the target officer gets a *counseling notice* versus being *terminated* for a sustained violation of sleeping on-duty would probably be less challenged. On the other hand, if the target officer is terminated for sleeping on-duty, it is more probable than not the penalty will be contested.

(2) Court Order

The jacket can be ordered released for whatever reasons the court determines appropriate. Occasionally an internal affairs file is released through this means. However, the entity the officer(s) has employed beforehand usually puts up a vigorous defense with the purpose of blocking the release. Additionally, this is one of those rare occasions when the police union and a public agency work together (not literally) to prevent the release of an officer's internal affairs file.

Usually when an attorney seeks an internal affairs file the court will review the file "in camera" (meaning privately in chambers) to determine what if any material in the file is relevant to the matter before the court. An example of this can be found in an officer who is being civilly sued for excessive use of force and the plaintiff's attorney wants the officer's internal affairs files to see if there are any other allegations similar to the plaintiff's cause.

(3) Order from Prosecutor/Attorney General

For reasons sometimes not provided, the Attorney General or Prosecutor order the internal affairs file to be turned over to their office. Under such an order, the file is releasable. The release of the file is standard practice when a complainant files a complaint with the Prosecutor or Attorney General's office because of their dissatisfaction with the local police department's findings.

(4) **Accompanying / Associated Lawsuit**

If or when a lawsuit is filed before, during, or after an internal affairs investigation, the completed investigation is releasable to the lawyers who are hired to defend the police department and officers in the legal action.

If the lawsuit is filed first, the lawsuit would serve as notification to the Chief and an internal affairs investigation should take place.

The unspoken fifth time when an internal affairs file is releasable, but probably not without legal intervention, is when the Chief is directed by his superiors to turn over the internal affairs files. Similar to the number two reason for release, the police union will likely join forces with the Chief in refuting the release of the internal affairs file(s); however, the Chief answers to a higher authority and under these circumstances when his boss orders the release of the file, the Chief's failure and/or refusal to follow the order could be a chargeable offense under, at minimum, insubordination. Described best in one New Jersey Office of Administrative Law case whereby the Chief of Police was demoted to Deputy Chief of Police, where they held, "in keeping with the paramilitary organization that [the Chief] ran. His failure to [comply] simply cannot be tolerated. [The Chief's] deliberate with-holding of files on one pretext or another, despite requests and orders to make these files available, created an untenable situation," *Palamara v. Township of Irvington*, OAL DKT. NO. CSV 3768-02 (May 9, 2003). Immediately after being ordered, the Chief should seek advice from the Prosecutor or Attorney General, but unless an injunction is granted by a court (before the date of release is expected) the order may need to be followed and grieved thereafter.

A File

In relationship to an officer's file, it is ill advised for the department to maintain or permit any more than one file on every officer. In other words, there should be one, and only one, personnel file. The personnel file would contain such things as the officer's payroll records, attendance sheets, training records, assignments, promotions, awards, certifications, and so on. In the interest of confidentiality, the officer's personnel file should be held by the Chief, unless the public entities

Personnel Manual dictates otherwise. Additional files maintained by the Chief include a medical file that contains all the officer's medical and psychological records and the officer's internal affairs file that holds all departmental discipline and investigations whereby the officer is/was the target. **What is commonplace, but should be discouraged, is for example, sergeants keeping a *Supervisor's file* on every officer in their squad. This is frowned on for several reasons, a few of which follow:**

- What the sergeant has in his file on an officer in his squad may be different from what the internal affairs commander has in the central depository regarding discipline;

- Statutes, case law, or collective bargaining agreements many times dictate when specific disciplinary action is removed and sometimes destroyed. If the sergeant does not remove and/or destroy a record the officer may have cause for action or a possible unfair labor practice charge; and

- If the sergeant's file is handed over to another sergeant on reassignment, the transfer of the file could be in violation of the officer's confidentiality rights, the rights under the collective bargaining agreement, and, depending on the contents, may give the officer a cause for action.

Chapter 9

Garrity Rights

> *We conclude that policemen, like teachers and lawyers, are not relegated to a watered-down version of constitutional rights.* **Garrity v. State of New Jersey**, 385 US 493 (1967)

Garrity Rights, also known as *Garrity Rule, Garrity Advisement, Garrity Law*, and *Garrity Warning*, is based on a case out of New Jersey where a Chief of Police (i.e., Garrity), four police officers (i.e., Officer Virtue of Bellmawr and Officer's Holroyd, Elwell, and Murray with Barrington), and Bellmawr's municipal court clerk (Mrs. Naglee) were suspected of traffic ticket fixing.

This case was unusually set off by New Jersey's Supreme Court who charged New Jersey's Attorney General to conduct the investigation, make inquiries, and investigate the allegations accordingly; the results of which were to be reported back to the Court. "Subsequent investigations produced evidence that the petitioners, in separate conspiracies, had falsified municipal court records, altered traffic tickets, and diverted moneys produced from bail and fines to unauthorized purposes." *Id.* at 502.

Before being asked any questions, the five police officers[13] were told their statements could be used against them in any criminal charges and warned that they could be terminated if they refused to answer the questions. As an example, Garrity and others were advised in part:

> *This right or privilege which you have is somewhat limited to the extent that you as a police officer under the laws of our state, may be subjected to a proceeding to have you removed from office if you refuse to answer a question put to you under oath pertaining to your office or your function within that office. It doesn't mean, however, you can't exercise the right. You do have the right. Footnote in* **Garrity**.

Simply put, the police officers were placed in an inescapable position of either answering the questions presented by the Deputy Attorney General and having their answers used against them criminally or not answering, which would have cost them their jobs.

---

[13] Mrs. Naglee's warning did not include the threat of losing her job if she refused to answer.

While Garrity, Virtue, and Naglee did not have a lawyer present during questioning, the three officers with Barrington did. Statements were initially provided and then months later, after not receiving the threat of termination for their failure to answer, another statement was taken, which for all intents and purposes echoed their initial statements. (All were told the second time they had the right to remain silent.) In addition to their statements, they all testified during their trials; thus, giving testimony that mirrored their earlier accounts.

Bear in mind, before January 16, 1967 that the *Garrity Rule* did not exist; therefore, all five officers in facing a true fear of losing their jobs answered the questions without immunity. As followed, some of their answers were used against the officers[14] in criminal charges and they were convicted in separate jury trials, which were ultimately affirmed[15] by New Jersey's Supreme Court.

Pursuant to Supreme Court *Rules*, a petition for a writ of certiorari was granted whereby the issue before them was whether in opposition to the Fifth and Fourteenth Amendments[16] a state, like New Jersey, can threaten a police officer with termination from their employment should the officer refuse to answer questions where their answers may incriminate them. Additionally, whether their statements were admissible as voluntary or "involuntary as a matter of law," *Id.* at 503, taking into account the Bellmawr employees did not have lawyers present during questioning, giving the impression they did not want attorneys. (Garrity himself voluntarily assisted in the preparation of his own interrogation.)

Sixty-five months after the first statement was taken, Justice Douglas on January 16, 1967, delivered the opinion for the United States Supreme Court holding "the protection of the individual under the Fourteenth Amendment against coerced statements prohibits use in subsequent criminal proceedings of statements obtained under threat of removal from office, and that it extends to all, whether they are policemen or other members of our body politic." *Id.* at 500.

As fundamental as this decision may seem to prosecutors, chiefs, and police officers today, the decision was not unanimous; whereby, four Justices dissented. (Judge White opined New Jersey's decision

---

[14] Mrs. Naglee had died.

[15] Cases were consolidated.

[16] "No State shall make or enforce any law which shall abridge the privileges or immunities of citizens of the United States; nor shall any State deprive any person of life, liberty, or property, without due process of law; nor deny to any person within its jurisdiction the equal protection of the laws."

should not be overturned.) The bases for the dissents were grounded in the voluntariness of the police officers' statements; hence, a position still argued today and that is slowly being chipped away. Knowing how close the decision actually was along with Justice White's dissent in agreeing with New Jersey's Supreme Court, target officers certainly should not casually walk into an interview and assume current protections today will be as valid tomorrow. The target should always keep in the back of his mind that anything's possible and what's good law today may not be good law tomorrow, because arguments surrounding *Miranda, Garrity*, and their equivalent are constantly challenged on a variety of grounds.

Two-prong Test

To avoid straying too far from *Garrity*, later courts provided guidance with respect to the application of *Garrity* where statements are concerned. First, the questions asked and answers provided need to be "specifically, directly, and narrowly relat[ed] to the performance of [the officer's] official duties," *Gardner v. Broderick*, 392 U.S. 273 (1968), and if and when given the officer "must have in fact believed [their] statements to be compelled on threat of loss of job and this belief must have been objectively reasonable," *United States v. Friedrick*, 842 F.2d 382, 395 (D.C.Cir. 1998). Simplified:

— Did the officer personally believe he was required to give a statement under the threat of losing his job?

— Was the officer's personal belief rational under the circumstances before him?

Self-executing

Unbeknownst to many, including police officers, the Fifth Amendment privilege "is not a self-executing mechanism; it can be affirmatively waived, or lost by not asserting it in a timely fashion," *Maness v. Meyers*, 419 U.S. 449 (1975); however, it can be asserted "in any proceeding, civil or criminal, administrative or judicial, investigatory or adjudicatory," *Kastigar v. United States*, 406 U.S. 441 (1972).

If the government grants Garrity (see *Garrity Rights Form* below) to compel an individual's testimony, then not only are the statements and testimony granted use immunity, but any evidence resulting from those statements are exempt as well. *Id.* at 441.

Garrity Rights Form

(1) I am being questioned as part of an investigation by this agency into potential violations of departmental rules and regulations, or for my fitness for duty. This investigation concerns _____.

(2) I have invoked my Miranda rights on the grounds that I might incriminate myself in this matter.

(3) I have been granted use immunity. No answer given by me, nor evidence derived from my answer, may be used against me in any criminal proceeding, except for perjury of false swearing.

(4) I understand that I must now answer questions specifically, directly, and narrowly related to the performance of my official duties or my fitness for office.

(5) If I refuse to answer, I may be subject to discipline for that refusal which can result in dismissal from this agency.

(6) Anything I say may be used against me in any subsequent department charges.

(7) I have the right to consult with a representative of my collective bargaining unit, or representative of my choice, and have him/her present during the interview.

For Example: A police officer wearing his uniform (i.e., navy blue pants (no stripe) and uniform shirt (covered with a jacket)) walks into a bank on his way to work and holds it up. While the officer is running out the door, he drops his departmental keys to the back door, locker, etc., which by policy needs to be on the officer at all times while on-duty. During muster that morning an inspection is done and the officer is questioned by the Captain, in front of the other officers, where his keys are. The officer pleads the "Fifth," which baffles the Captain, but since it also called into question his authority he screams at the officer and orders him to answer the question or be fired. The officer again pleads the Fifth, this time making the Captain angrier and now compelling him to respond. The officer asks, "Are you compelling me to answer?" The Captain responds, "Yes." The officer then tells the Captain his keys were dropped this morning at the bank that he robbed. In this case, the defense attorney will argue the statement made by the officer and the keys cannot be used against the officer in any criminal proceedings.

This example offers several key points:

(1) The officer requested the *Fifth Amendment* protection. That is, *Garrity Rights* have to be invoked by the officer because the *Fifth Amendment* is not self-executing, and

(2) The officer cannot grant himself use immunity, and

(3) The employer can trigger use immunity by compelling an officer to answer questions under the threat of being discharged and/or fired.

Therefore, training needs to take place ensuring that employers or their representatives are educated enough to refrain from forcing an officer to answer questions under the threat of being disciplined or terminated. On the other hand, union representatives over the years have instructed their members to insert the following sample paragraph on all submitted statements:

> *It is my understanding that this report is made for administrative, internal police department purposes only and will not be used as part of an official investigation. This report is made by me after being ordered to do so by lawful supervisory officers. It is my understanding that by refusing to obey an order to write this report that I can be disciplined for insubordination and that the punishment for insubordination can be up to and including termination of employment. This report is made only pursuant to such orders and potential punishment/discipline that can result from failure to obey that order.*

It is this paragraph that gives the officer the belief their statements cannot be used against them in any criminal proceedings. Considering it is possible the insertion of this paragraph may in some way grant the officer use immunity and the prosecutor or attorney general are the only ones empowered to grant use immunity, no statements should be accepted by the investigator with this paragraph affixed. Taking into account the officer inserts the waiver with the understanding his words are immune, the investigator should acknowledge the officer is invoking his Fifth Amendment rights, but the investigator should not accept the report. Under these circumstances, it is not unreasonable to tell the target officer to submit the report without the above statement, because the investigator does not want to give the officer any false sense of security or the wrong impression regarding the use of his statement.

Waiving Immunity—NOT!

These sequence of events are unfortunately very commonplace:

- A police officer is a suspect in a criminal act, and

- Immediately after the Internal Affairs Investigator asks the first question the target officer pleads the Fifth. In other words, the target officer refuses to waive his immunity from criminal prosecution.

Ask yourself, what should the investigator do next? Should he,

(1) Compel the target to answer under threat of being disciplined or fired?

(2) Stop the questioning and confirm or deny whether the Prosecutor or Attorney General will grant *Garrity*?

(3) Stop the questioning and investigate without a statement?

Considering, as discussed, that a police officer does not have watered-down rights, it should be apparent by now that option 1 is not the best choice or, for that matter, not a viable choice at all; therefore, what's left are options 2 and 3.

While a majority of investigators in a majority of investigations would stop the questioning and try to get the Prosecutor to grant *Garrity*, this option should unquestionably be the last choice. This option is frequently picked first, because it saves the investigator time and also typically discloses information he may not have known about before. However, the problem with allowing a target officer to spoon-feed information to the investigator is that he could deceptively lead an investigation down the wrong path. Contrary to a good trial lawyer's way of thinking that he would "never ask a question that he don't already know the answer to," when *Garrity* is given to a target officer it generally means the investigator either stopped short of overturning every single stone connected to the allegation or has overturned every possible stone and in the end has nothing left. If the reason for granting *Garrity* to the target is the latter, it is obvious the evidence within the jacket will not support moving forward with charges and merely relying on the target's statement to secure disciplinary action is not in the agency's best interest. Stated differently, if all the investigator has to sustain an allegation is the target officer's own statement, the Chief needs to think twice before he files any charges. On the other hand, if the reason for granting *Garrity* is because the investigator did not conduct a thorough investigation, the target's questioning was premature and the investigator needs to dig a lot deeper.

That said, the bottom line is to only seek *Garrity* for the target officer if and when the unknown information the investigator receives will further the investigation of another officer and not the target officer personally or with the understanding that the penalty will not be what it would have been if the investigation collected substantial material evidence before the target received *Garrity*.

Nonetheless, whenever a target officer takes the Fifth, all questioning must stop and will not start again unless the officer either waives immunity or is granted *Garrity*. **Though at this point in time it is important to set forth two important points:**

(1) Police officers who are the target of a criminal investigation should never waive their immunity without the advice of a competent labor attorney who specializes in police misconduct. (There it is said, but even after officers read this, there will be cops out there who will waive their immunity without even consulting an attorney.) Internal affairs investigators, for the most part, will only use the target's words against the target to corroborate the evidence they already gathered. From an internal affairs investigator's point of view, the more the target gives the investigator the easier the investigation will be to bring to a conclusion, but if a target officer believes that if he just gives his side of the story to the investigator, the matter will go away or the officer will be cleared of any wrongdoing, in most cases, he is mistaken.

(2) The Chief needs to know that when an officer "refuse[s] to answer questions specifically, directly, and narrowly related to

the performance of [her] official duties, without being required to waive [her] immunity with respect to the use of [her] answers or the fruits thereof in a criminal prosecution of [her]self, ... the privilege against self-incrimination would not have been a bar to [her] dismissal," *Gardner v. Broderick*, 392 U.S. 273, 278 (1968). To be precise, disciplining a target officer up to and including termination is warranted if based on all credible evidence collected it provides sufficient evidence to file appropriate charges.

Garrity's Purpose

Garrity is an excellent tool to be used if and when witnesses who possess information on a criminal investigation, refuse to waive immunity, and the information they possess can be used against another officer in a more significant investigation. Many times, if not most, the witnesses' statements do not tend to incriminate themselves; still, since the witnesses are not absolutely sure their statements may or may not serve to incriminate themselves, they seek immunity. *Garrity* is commonly offered to witnesses for administrative investigations as well as criminal investigations; therefore, it is not the level of the charges that dictate the request for *Garrity*, but the alleged information the witness possesses.

Cautiously, the words written on the line "This investigation concerns ____" cannot be inserted nonchalantly and must be carefully chosen as to not indirectly give an officer immunity for something not relevant to the case before the investigator.

Case in point: An officer is under investigation for suspicion of on-line illegal betting. After a forensic search of the officer's computer nothing is found, closes the criminal investigation and opens an administrative one. However, through ineptness, the prosecutor inserted the vague phrase "computer misuse" on the blank *Garrity Rights Form* line. Before questioning, the target requests and is handed the *Garrity Rights Form* and *Administrative Investigation Only Form* for "computer misuse." During questioning, the officer proffers he was using the computer illegally, but it wasn't on-line illegal betting he was doing, he was downloading child pornography and it was on another unexamined department computer. Although this officer could be charged departmentally and dismissed for downloading child pornography, his statement, acts, and the computer (i.e., fruit of a poisonous tree) are probably all lost evidence in a criminal prosecution. The more specific caption listed on both forms should have been something like "illegal betting," this way once the target started proffering spontaneous utterances regarding child pornography or anything else that hinted on criminality, the investigator would stop the questioning and read the target his Miranda Rights.

Once *Garrity* is given to the witness, it is highly recommended that the witness is then given a *Witness Acknowledgement Form.*

WITNESS ACKNOWLEDGEMENT FORM

1. I acknowledge that I have been informed that I am a witness in a supervisory investigation. This investigation concerns suspected

    _____.

2. I acknowledge my responsibility to answer truthfully all questions specifically related to the performance of my official duties.

3. I acknowledge that this investigation is confidential, and I am hereby ordered not to disclose any information discussed throughout the process.

4. If I answer "I don't recall" or its equivalent to any question— within 12 hours upon recall I will document the answers to the investigators attention.

5. Any new information received, relating to this investigation, shall be immediately documented to the investigators attention.

Name: Date:

Signature:

Witness:

Although the purpose behind this form is important, there are three specific ones that need to be pointed out: *first*, it confirms for the witness that he indeed is a witness and not the target of the investigation; *second*, it officially places the witness on notice that any information that comes to light after the interview shall be immediately brought to the investigator's attention; and *third*, it inhibits the reluctant witness who anticipates falling back on "I don't recall" with the purpose of placing as much distance as possible between their damaging facts and the thin blue line.

Offering *Garrity* to the target officer is not the optimum move but, when definitely needed, it should be followed up with an *Administrative Investigation Only Form.*

ADMINISTRATIVE INVESTIGATION ONLY FORM

1. I am being questioned as part of an investigation by this agency into potential violations of department rules and regulations, or for my fitness for duty. This investigation concerns_____.

2. This is an administrative investigation. I will be asked questions specifically, narrowly, and directly related to the performance of my official duties.

3. I may be subject to departmental discipline for refusing to answer a question directly related to the performance of my duties or for not answering truthfully.

4. I have the right to consult with a representative of my collective bargaining unit, or another representative of my choice and have my representative present during the interview or have my representative review my completed "white sheet" prior to turning it in.

5. If I answer "I don't recall" or its equivalent to any question—upon recall I will document the answers to the investigators attention.

6. Any new information received, relating to this investigation, shall be immediately documented to the investigators attention.

Signature:

Date: Time:

Witnessed by:

Like the *Witness Acknowledgement Form*, the *Administrative Investigation Only Form* serves a constructive purpose. It too places the target officer on notice that if any information comes to light after the interview he is departmentally obligated, through this order, to bring the information to the investigator's attention. This is very important because it will eliminate the target officer's legal representative from bringing up any surprises in the future; and if they do, the target officer could be subsequently charged with insubordination. Again, like the *Witness* form, any "I don't recall" answers or its equivalent provided by the target during the interview will require immediate notification if and when his memory improves. This form also serves as the target's confirmation that he will only be asked questions that are "specifically, narrowly, and directly related to the performance of [their] official duties," and his refusal to answer could result in him being disciplined. He is made aware that he needs to be truthful in all responses, and all information may be used against him in departmental charges. He is also entitled to a representative if he so chooses.

Therefore, all in all, it is important to remember several things with regards to *Garrity*:

(1) Any statements made after invoking *Garrity* may only be used for departmental investigation purposes and not for criminal prosecution purposes;

(2) The officer must announce that he wants the protections under *Garrity*, because it is not automatic when questioning is taking place;

(3) Before *Garrity* is given, it shall be reviewed and approved by the County Prosecutor or Assistant Prosecutor (signed off by legal review);

(4) *Garrity* should be in writing, be very specific to the immunity given, and the officer should be given a copy; and

(5) The officer cannot rely on *Garrity* when the target of an investigation is internal and not criminal.

Chapter 10
Weingarten Rights

If this interview could in any way lead to my being disciplined or terminated, or affect my personal working conditions, I respectfully request that my union representative or attorney be present during questioning.

Background and Procedural History

Amazingly so, the rights guaranteed under *Weingarten* all started over $1.98 worth of chicken. By way of background, Weingarten is a retail store that had a lunch counter where union member Leura Collins worked. There was an allegation filed against Collins that she paid only $1 for a box of chicken that could hold $2.98 worth. Weingarten placed Collins under surveillance and eventually called her in for an investigatory interview. Once called in, Collins requested a union representative, but Weingarten denied her request; therefore, she provided a statement that she used the $2.98 box, but only purchased $1 worth of chicken. Collins claimed the $2.98 boxes were not available, which Weingarten confirmed was accurate and apologized accordingly.

It was during Collins' initial statement to Weingarten that they realized she admitted to getting free lunches. After researching this, Weingarten determined that the retail store did not have a clear policy on giving free lunches to employees so they decided to interview Collins. Again Collins requested a union representative and again Weingarten denied her request; however, this time they also advised her that she could not discuss this matter with anyone, thus prompting the union to file an unfair labor practice charge against Weingarten.

The National Labor Relations Board ruled in favor of Collins, holding that Weingarten violated the National Labor Relations Act, *J. Weingarten, Inc.*, 202 NLRB 446 (1973). Weingarten appealed the case; whereby, the Court of Appeals for the Fifth Circuit ruled in favor of *Weingarten*, 485 F. 2d 1135 (1973), followed by the United States Supreme Court's granting certiorari.

In *NLRB v. J. Weingarten, Inc.*, 420 US 251 (1975) Supreme Court Justice Brennan delivered the opinion for the Court, which held that while many collective bargaining agreements already address an employee's right to representation during investigatory interviews, if an agreement is silent on said representation it is not unreasonable for an employee to have a union representative present when the employee reasonably believes the outcome of the interview may result in discipline.

Application

In applying the Supreme Court's decision, an internal affairs investigator should begin with understanding the definition of an investigatory interview. Simply stated, an investigatory interview is one in which the investigator brings an officer in and questions him to obtain information specifically, directly, and narrowly related to his official position where he has reason to believe discipline may result off the exchange. It is the officer's right to have a union representative present if he believes the interview may result in disciplinary action. Additionally, like an officer's *Garrity* rights, an officer's *Weingarten* rights are also not self-executing; therefore, if the officer does not ask for a union representative before or during questioning, they are not automatically entitled to one. (An officer cannot be disciplined for making this request.)

If an officer exercises his *Weingarten* rights and asks to have a union representative present throughout his investigatory interview, the internal affairs investigator has four options:

(1) The investigator can grant the officer's request. If so, the investigator should immediately stop all questioning and reassume only when the union representative is present.

(2) The investigator can deny the officer's request. If so, the investigator should immediately stop all questioning.

(3) The investigator can give the officer a choice: Conduct the investigatory interview without the union representative present or terminate the investigatory interview.

(4) The investigator can deny the officer's request, but instead of stopping the investigatory interview, he continues to question the officer. This course of action is not recommended and the union could view it as an unfair labor practice violation on behalf of the employer and file the appropriate charges. Furthermore, it is highly probable that any and all statements that come after the continued investigatory interview cannot be used against the officer to support administrative disciplinary charges.

Prior to broadly applying employee rights like *Weingarten* to every officer uniformly, it is essential the particular collective bargaining agreement covering the specific officer being called in for an investigatory interview is reviewed for supplemental rights. An example of one of these rights not explicitly addressed in *Weingarten* is who can serve as the officer's union representative. This individual or individuals are generally defined in the agreement and can include an attorney of the officer's choosing, an attorney chosen by the union, or anyone the union believes will best represent the officer. Understand, the union representative could actually be the target officer's mother[17] if that is who the union believes is in the officer's best interest.

Other important things generally negotiated in the collective bargaining agreements include the amount of notice (i.e., time) the officer and union will receive before an investigatory interview will take place. If the investigatory interview will be videotaped, audio recorded, and if White Sheets or a stenographer will be used to record the officer's official statements. (It goes without saying, if the collective bargaining agreement calls for the use of a stenographer and the investigator only audio records the statement, then the use of the statement will probably be barred by the hearing officer.)

Outside of the officer's collective bargaining agreement, the investigator needs to be familiar with any rights established in the entity's Personnel Policy/Manual, Ordinances, and Resolutions as well as federal and state laws and regulations.

Witnesses

The prior discussion intentionally did not separate target from witness regarding an officer's *Weingarten* rights. This is so, because even if an officer receives a *Witness Acknowledgement Form* once he has reason to believe his statements could result in discipline, he would be entitled to union representation, but not unless he asks for it. (An excellent investigator realizes he only knows what he knows; because what he *thinks* or *believes* he knows is not what he knows he knows.) Not knowing what will come out of the mouth of the witness, it is unreasonable for the investigator to prohibit an officer from having a union representative, but the witness officer should be placed on notice that arbitrarily requesting a representative without cause will be examined for departmental violations and/or obstruction of an official police investigation.

---

[17] Don't lose sight of the fact that the officer's mother could also be an attorney.

Weingarten, Not Applicable

Knowing when *Weingarten* applies is important to ensure the proper protection of the law enforcement officer's rights, but knowing when it is not applicable is important to avoid creating a practice not established by agreement, or required by statute or case law.

There are times when the internal affairs investigator collects evidence and interviews witnesses, but does not interview the target officer, although this is not considered the proper way to conduct a thorough investigation against someone who wears a blue uniform. If the target officer is not being interviewed and is only being served with the predetermined charges, there is no lawful reason to grant *Weingarten* rights to the target during the service of those charges. This same principle applies to a target after an investigatory interview (with or without a union representative) during the service of disciplinary charges.

Furthermore, but certainly the most unwise, is when an internal affairs investigator conducts an interview with no intention of disciplining the target officer. Many times this practice is used for police officers who are witnesses, but even under these circumstances the investigator needs to be cautious, because what the witness knows remains unknown until the interview. Regardless of the preconceived notion to not discipline off of an officer's statement, procedurally the investigator would start the interview with a statement to the officer that "this interview is not investigatory, but informative only; therefore, no discipline will come from your statement." From that point forward, it is unmistakable the officer has no *Weingarten* right to a union representative during the interview or for that matter any predetermined disciplinary action that follows.

Aside from the investigatory interview there are other times when *Weingarten* rights would not apply. These include, but are not limited to, any physical or psychological examinations; breath samples; blood samples, voice recognition, handwriting samples; hair samples; and saliva samples. Although an acceptable practice for almost four decades, lineups are just starting to become a topic of consideration; therefore, it is noteworthy to mention that in *Biehunik v. Felicetta*, 441 F.2d 228 (2d Cir.), cert. denied, 403 U.S. 932 (1971), the Second Circuit upheld a procedure in which sixty-two police officers were forced to appear in a lineup for purposes of identification by persons who claimed they were assaulted by a police officer, quoting *Kirkpatrick v. City of Los Angeles*, 803 F.2d 485, 488 (9th Cir. 1986). The court in support of their decision stated:

A trustworthy police force is a precondition of minimal social stability in our imperfect society, a fact repeatedly dramatized by tragic incidents of violent conflict between police and some groups of civilians that continue to break out periodically in so many of our cities. Moreover, it is a correlative of the public's right to minimize the chance of police misconduct that policeman, who voluntarily accept the unique status of watchman of the social order, may not reasonably expect the same freedom from governmental restraints which are designed to ensure his fitness for office as from similar governmental actions not so designed. The policeman's employment relationship by its nature implies that in certain aspects of his affairs, he does not have the full privacy and liberty from police officials that he would otherwise enjoy. **Biehunik**, *supra at 230–31.*

Role of the Union Representative

More contentious than whether or not the officer is entitled to a union representative is what role the union representative will serve during an investigatory interview. If the investigator understands and accepts that his two primary functions are to protect an officer's rights and at the same time open-mindedly gather all pertinent material facts regardless of what direction the evidence takes him, then the role of the union representative should not be as controversial as it is.

Realizing there's a continuous balance between protecting the officer's rights and the need to collect facts, a competent union representative should seek to clarify some relevant facts, ask for a question to be repeated, or seek clarification on an investigator's questions; they should be welcomed as long as the frequency of interruption does not become excessive and purposefully distracting. This would also include the representative offering supplemental knowledge another officer may possess that could assist in the furtherance of the case.

Basically, it is the role of the union representative to provide assistance to the officer, but he is not permitted to interfere, and at any time the investigator can insist the only response he wants to listen to is that of the officer. Furthermore, at no time should a union representative's attendance transform the investigatory interview into a negotiation session debating the interpretation of the officer's collective bargaining agreement or an adversarial relationship that will eventually get in the way (sometimes purposeful) of the actual objective of the interview. It is undisputed that the investigator maintains a legitimate cause in uncovering the facts and any inappropriate interference cannot be tolerated.

Chapter 11
Loudermill Rights

The issue plainly presented before the court was "what pre-termination process must be accorded a public employee who can be discharged only for cause," *Cleveland Bd. of Ed. v. Loudermill*, 470 U.S. 532, 535 (1985) for which they opined that due process requires "some kind of hearing" before an employer can terminate an employee who possesses a property interest in his employment; holding,

> *The essential requirements of due process ... are notice and an opportunity to respond. The opportunity to present reasons, either in person or in writing, why proposed action should not be taken is a fundamental due process requirement.... The tenured employee is entitled to oral or written notice of the charges against him, and explanation of the employer's evidence and an opportunity to present his side of the story...,* Id. at 541–46.

By and large, probationary police officers are not covered by *Loudermill* unless the probationary officer is let go before their training period comes up for permanency. However, excepting probationary officers, regular permanent police officers who are tenured in their position possess a property or liberty interest in their employee/employer relationship. When tenure exists, the Chief is required to serve notice to the officer about what charges are being lodged and should include the sought after penalty.

If and when the suspected grounds behind the need to discipline warrant an immediate suspension to maintain the integrity of the police department and/or there are realistic safety concerns or the health of the officer or another is at risk, the decision needs to be made as to whether or not the suspension is with or without pay. If paid, other than the *Preliminary Notice of Discipline*, there is no need to conduct a *Loudermill* hearing, because there is no liberty or property loss. Included with the Preliminary Notice of Discipline, when suspended, there should be a suspension notice. **A suspension notice should have, at least, the following directives worded in the best interest of the agency:**

(1) The officer shall immediately turn in all department-issued service weapon(s), all police badges, police identifications, all police communication equipment, all keys, computer hardware and software, and all other police department property currently in the officer's possession.

83

(2) The officer shall reveal, list, and itemize all passwords related to the use, operation, and maintenance of any computer hardware/software.

(3) The officer shall be ordered to not identify himself or represent himself in public as a member of the department; unless he also points out he is on suspension. (An officer on an unpaid suspension that identifies himself as a police officer without the fact that he's on suspension could be investigated for impersonating.)

(4) The officer shall be reminded that he remains under the lawful control of the department and is subject to the department's policies.

(5) The officer shall be prohibited from entering the police department unless advanced approval is provided by the Chief or with a lawful reason for him to be there (e.g., officer is victim).

(6) The officer shall be prohibited from communicating with any officers during their working hours. (The other officers should be made aware that they are prohibited from communicating with any officer on suspension during their on-duty hours.)

(7) The officer shall be directed that while on suspension he is prohibited from requesting any police officer for copies of police records. All requests shall be made either through the Chief, *Open Public Records Act* or the *Freedom of Information Act*.

When changing an officer's employment status from a paid to an unpaid suspension or the officer is initially getting suspended without pay, the Chief needs to provide the officer with a *Loudermill* hearing. **Taking direction from our courts, prior to any unpaid suspension the officer shall...**

- ... receive notice of the suspension. If possible, this notice is best if in writing followed by a face-to-face explanation, and

- ... be given an opportunity to respond. An acceptable response should be limited to the officer's rationale as to why he does not believe a suspension without pay is justified.

Once the officer receives notice and is given an opportunity to offer his explanation, the obligations as required under *Loudermill* are complete; thus, leaving the final decision up to the Chief as to whether the initial thought of suspending without pay stands. If the suspension without pay stands, the Chief institutes the suspension and hand delivers to him the immediate suspension notice (as discussed above) if he had not already received the notice in connection to a paid suspension.

Whether to suspend or not and whether the suspension will be paid or unpaid are difficult decisions to render when the Chief inserts compassion in the equation; therefore, the decision has to be based only on what is in the best interest of the department. It should be understood that if the officer is suspended with pay and is found guilty he should be required to pay the tax dollars (e.g., salary and benefits) back on a case-by-case basis, and if unpaid the public entity should reimburse the suspended officer for all lost salary and benefits; therefore, whatever final decision is made cannot be made haphazardly and needs to be carefully thought out.

That said, a common suspension with pay in which public entities do not seek reimbursement is when the Chief suspects the officer is psychologically unfit-for-duty and the officer is suspended with pay pending a medical professional's evaluation. However, suspensions with pay in which the officer is found guilty of insubordination, neglect of duty, oath violations, and so on could warrant a serious cost factor analysis between the reimbursement amount(s) versus legal representation.

Conversely, a Chief almost always has the option of not suspending the subject officer and instead having him report to work. This officer, conditional on why the suspension was considered to begin with, could be reassigned to dispatch, records, evidence (without access to weapons), and so on. This option is implemented by large agencies but is frowned upon by smaller ones, because once the Chief permits an officer to be placed on restricted duty they may have to accommodate all officers in similar circumstances. This could be troubling if a small department is compelled to accommodate more officers than it has supplemental assignments.

A third option, depending on the circumstances, would be reassigning the officer to another job function within the municipality (e.g., Road Department); however, this is rarely done without the cooperation of the union, officer, and the employees of the department reassigned.

Considering these options, the Chief and labor attorney should weigh:

(1) The police department's chances of success on the forthcoming charges,

(2) The time frame before the case is settled,

(3) Possible reassignment options, both inside and outside the police department,

(4) The public entities impact financially and otherwise,

(5) Reimbursement factors.

Experience has shown that, on average, no matter what decision the powers that be make concerning an officer who is unready or unable to perform their law enforcement responsibilities (e.g., suspend with pay, suspend without pay, or reassignment), it is highly probable a third of the public will accept it, a third will not accept it, and the remaining third will be neutral; therefore, the initial decision will be realistically a financial one ultimately becoming thereafter an emotional one.

Chapter 12
Free Speech

A New Jersey police chief recently "stood at the microphone during the public portion of the ... Council meeting Thursday night with a miniature skeleton, a basket filled with dirty laundry and a little plastic house." Using the props to emphasize his point, the chief "told them they had plenty of dirty laundry,... that people in glass houses shouldn't throw stones...[a]nd there was a skeleton in their closet."[18] A Pennsylvania officer was suspended with pay over his alleged "pro-fanity-laced off-duty rant in which he talks about [a victim] who died ... of a gunshot to the head outside the bar."[19] A former South Dakota police officer is suing to get his job back after he was fired "for comments he made at a grievance hearing for another police department employee."[20] Former Texas College Station Police Chief, Michael Clancey, was fired "when he dared to suggest that the College Station City Council should not use red light cameras as a budgetary tool,"[21] and another officer in New Jersey was under investigation after a CD containing what is described in published reports as "a raunchy comedy act" was mailed to police officials.

Although miles apart, these officers and hundreds more across the United States continue to face charges over the debate of what is and what is not an exercise of an officer's right of free speech. That is, does the fundamental importance of these officers free speech rights ensure they maintain a right of free expression even if their actions are unpopular? What is certain is that our Constitution and the courts have not eliminated a police officer's First Amendment right to comment publically on matters of public concern. See *Connick v. Myers*, 461 U.S. 138 (1983); however, the cloudiness in where the line is drawn continues to be open to a difference of opinion. That is, while the First Amendment protects a citizen's rights, but the interpretation of where the line is crossed for a police officer who is speaking as a citizen on an issue of public concern, will, for the most part, be left to an outsider only after an officer believes they have been wronged.

---

[18] http://www.northjersey.com/towns/Mayor_Police_chiefs_statements_uncalled_for_and_unfounded.html

[19] http://wcbstv.com/national/James.Cousins.caught.2.988779.html

[20] http://www.keloland.com/NewsDetail6162.cfm?Id=0,100442

[21] http://www.thetruthaboutcars.com/texas-police-Chief-fired-for-questioning-red-light-cameras/

When founding father James Madison proposed the *Bill of Rights* in 1789, he unwaveringly believed that:

> *Congress shall make no law respecting an establishment of religion, or prohibiting the free exercise thereof; or abridging the freedom of speech, or of the press; or the right of the people peaceably to assemble, and to petition the Government for a redress of grievances.* **USCS Const. Amend. 1** ...

therefore, many Americans believe whatever action the government takes against a citizen based on their spoken words treads on Madison's thinking. Accordingly, our Supreme Court has granted "We the People" the right to even prohibit public officials from recovering from any damages "for a defamatory falsehood relating to his official conduct unless he proves that the statement was made with 'actual malice'— that is, with knowledge that it was false or with reckless disregard of whether it was false or not," *New York Times Co. v. Sullivan*, 376 U.S. 254 (1964).

As a result, have these decisions infringed on these officers' Constitutional Rights? Were they speaking as citizens who were merely addressing public concerns? The simple answer is *it depends* on which side you are on: The charging party believes the law enforcement officers' crossed the Rubicon and when they spoke publically on matters that were not public concerns and when they spoke they did so as public officials; the charged party believes they were speaking as citizens with public concerns. For assistance in answering these questions and more, the United States Supreme Court provided guidance to Police Chiefs in 2006 to determine if and when an officer's utterance is within the area of the Constitution's protected speech. Our justices held that "when public employees make statements pursuant to their official duties, the employees are not speaking as citizens for First Amendment purposes, and the Constitution does not insulate their communications from employer discipline," *Garcetti v. Ceballos*, 547 U.S. 410, 421 (2006). The *Garcetti* court further held, "First Amendment does not prohibit managerial discipline based on an employee's expressions made pursuant to official responsibilities." *Id.* at 425.

When applying *Garcetti* to an officer's speech, it is very important for the internal affairs investigator to focus on five questions:

(1) **What was official position of the speaker when the speech was made?**

A law enforcement officer can be in one of four possible official positions (i.e., sworn officer, private citizen, union member, and union official) when the comment is made. The member's position at the exact moment the speech is made needs to be resolved by the investigator. This determination cannot be left open to doubt; therefore, he can serve only one role, and if it is not clear which position he is in at the time then the position most favorable to the member shall be the one selected.[22]

Generally speaking, when no confidential information or records are disclosed, the most favorable positions are that of the union representative, private citizen, and union member the least favorable is that of sworn officer. During contract negotiations, again the union representative and union member are the most favorable and the sworn officer's position the least favorable. (A private citizen would not be applicable.) A police officer who works and resides in the same city who discusses community concerns publically[23] is the most favorable position, while speaking as a sworn officer is the least favorable. (A union representative or member would not be applicable.)

For the most part, union officials should be treated on an equal footing with their adversary when dealing with negotiations and grievances unless evidence dictates otherwise; therefore, in those types of settings, they are generally free to speak unrestricted on the working conditions, because they are representing the best interest of their membership and not acting in their official police officer positions. This argument would more than likely be taken up when a union official speaks publically (e.g., council meeting) if the subject matter pertains to the membership. Knowing this, if by happenstance an officer speaks publically and later claims he was acting as a union representative, his claim needs to be proven and not

---

[22] In balancing the position most favorable to the member it should be noted first that the scale is only with respect to Free Speech investigations; therefore depending on the subject matter and the supportive material the position on the scale could change.

[23] If his neighbors have just as much information as he possesses.

taken for granted. This defense is not uncommon, but can be confirmed by first listening to his opening statement (e.g., "Hi, I'm Virginia Dare, *President* of Local #148," assuming it is heard live or recorded. If there is no opening statement, there should be an Oath of Office for each Executive Board member coupled with official union minutes to verify a recorded motion, second, and vote. That is, can Virginia Dare provide proof to the internal affairs investigator that when he made his statement he did so in his official capacity as president of the union? As such, if a union official is critical of the chief and/or his actions, the investigator needs to determine if such criticism was stated outside the union official's duties as a police officer and if such criticisms either were disruptive or had a negative bearing on the department's outside relationships with other entities. As illustrated in *Bradley v. James*, 479 F. 3d 536, 538 (8th Circuit, 2007), whereby the court held, "[Bradley's] speech was pursuant to his official and professional duties" as a police captain. Here, only Bradley broached his allegations surrounding the chief during an inquiry from within the department; whereby, Bradley gave a statement while in his official police position. It is obvious that the only reason the captain was in a position to view the chief was because of his on-the-job duties, and if Bradley was a private citizen he probably would never have been in a position to observe anything. As in *Bradley*, the investigator would need to make a distinction between the exact role of the target officer and when the speech was made (i.e., citizen or public official) and whether or not the officer was speaking as a private citizen or a public official. Bradley was a police captain being interviewed as a police captain on a subject he was intimately aware of only because of his official position as a police captain; hence, his official duty clearly outweighed that of his rights as a private citizen. Interestingly, even if Bradley went to the media and reported the Chief's alleged intoxication he still would have been speaking as a public official, because the reason he has knowledge of the Chief's alleged intoxication is due only to his position as police captain and regardless of where his comments were made it is highly probable the court would have ruled the same way.

(2) **What environment was the speaker in when the speech was made?**

There are various locations where an officer can be when his speech is made. Some common places include, but are not limited to: council meeting; muster; union hall; and the bar. An important factor as it relates to where the comments were made is similar to real estate: *location, location, location.* Therefore, it is necessary to determine the officer's location, as well as who was present when the comments were made and who exactly heard it (see 5).

(3) **How did the speaker come into possession of the information?**

There is a plethora of public police records that are open to the people by way of the state's *Open Public Records Act, Common Law* right to access governmental records or the *Federal Freedom of Information Act.* These records, as the Acts refer, include, but are not limited to, all public records that civilians can gain access to by making a request to the public entity. While an officer has as much authority as a civilian to submit a request and obtain public police records, officers could have unfettered access to police reports depending on their assignments, which civilians are not permitted access to by law.

Therefore, an investigator needs to know which records are considered open to the public versus which records are not. Furthermore, if the records are open to the public, the investigator needs to determine whether or not the records were received through proper or improper channels. Equally, if the officer produces and openly discusses records that are accessible only through his official position, how he gained access to those records should be explored further.

Besides public records, police officers are continually privileged to information solely because, for example, they are the lead detective for an ongoing investigation or they are the Administrative Lieutenant responsible for budget preparation. Under these circumstances, the information this officer receives when connected to his official duties is confidential unless the release is authorized by a superior or by law.

Regardless of what records, information, or data are proffered by the officer, the investigator needs to look into whether or not the possession is legitimate. (Unlawful possession of records and/or disclosure of confidential information could amount to a separate case.) Make no mistake about it, the investigation may need to determine not only what records the officer possessed but also how the officer obtained those records.

(4) **Precisely, what did the speaker say?**
People mean what they say, and say what they mean; therefore, every single internal affairs investigator should take an advanced course in identifying deceptive behavior. If interviewing with White Sheets the investigator needs to be educated in statement analysis (i.e., written), and if interviewing on audio or video the investigator needs to be educated in a verbal/non-verbal communications course (e.g., *Identifying Deceptive Behavior on a Traffic Stop*). What the officer stated could make or break the case, so here is not a place to assume, cut corners, insert words for him or take anything for granted.

(5) **Who was the receiver of the speech?**
The investigator needs to take into consideration the audience hearing the speech. For instance, if comments are given to the Chief by his Deputy Chief at the Chief's request with the intent of providing strategic advice for the betterment of the agency it would be treated in a different manner than if the same Deputy Chief's comments were presented to the mayor and council during a public meeting and without the consent and knowledge of the Chief.

In summary, an investigator needs to thoroughly authenticate each of the above five answers and think of each answer as a piece of a larger puzzle. Separately the answers may lead an investigator nowhere or no closer to a conclusion; however, if all the pieces form an absolute conclusion that the officer's speech demoralizes the department and violates an officer's Oath of Office, then moving forward with disciplinary charges should be contemplated. Conversely, disciplining an officer when any or all of the pieces cast doubt as to whether or not an officer conclusively made a comment needs to be solidly rejected so as not to violate an officer's First Amendment rights.

When balancing *Garcetti* with an allegation, the internal affairs investigator should first look at the particular position the officer was in, followed by what his statement was, and exactly what information and/or records were used in relationship to his public comments.

Additionally, the investigator needs to eliminate any doubt as to whether the officer was speaking as a private citizen, which in most cases can be proved or disproved simply by analyzing (verbatim if possible) his words. Besides the officer's position at the time, special emphasis should be placed on what is said and how it relates to this officer's official position; e.g., detective during *choir practice*[24] and discusses the specifics of a homicide investigation he was on earlier that day with unsworn patrons within earshot.

If the police officer was not speaking as a citizen he would have a difficult time proving to the court that he has a First Amendment right. If the officer was not speaking on a matter of public concern, again, he would have a difficult time proving to the court he has a First Amendment right. However, if he was speaking as a citizen and what he was saying turned out to be a matter of public concern then the question is whether he was treated differently as compared to how the general public would be treated if they said the same thing (e.g., Did the Chief overreact to the officer's speech?). See *Pickering v. Board of Education*, 391 U.S. 563 (1968). Here the impartial internal affairs investigator is left to determine through all credible evidence gathered if, when the speech was made, the words expressed were made independent of the officer's official law enforcement position by answering no less than the five above questions. For that reason, once it is determined the officer's speech was made pursuant to his official capacity, either directly or indirectly, the investigator is then left to determine if and how it affected the agency. One example of how a public employee's comments could indirectly touch on the public agency warranting discipline occurred in New York where a volunteer firefighter was terminated after he publically complained about inadequate funding his department received in comparison to a neighboring fire department. After an investigation the Board suspended then expelled the firefighter based on their belief that the firefighter's letter "had had a 'detrimental impact' on the Fire Department and its relations with its neighboring fire departments," and the court upheld the termination. *McClernon v. Beaver Dams Volunteer Fire Department*, 489 F. Supp. 2d 291—Dist. Court, WD New York 2007. As *McClernon* points out, even if the impact does not directly affect the officer's agency, if an officer's words indirectly encroach on external relationships with other entities, discipline is not out of the question. Taking *McClernon* one step further, the Chief does not need to confirm a definite adverse effect on the department to discipline an

---

[24] Squad goes out after work (regardless of shift), drinks alcohol, and unwinds.

officer; hence, the Chief should not "allow events to unfold to the extent that the disruption of the office and the destruction of the working relationships is manifest before taking action." *Connick v. Myers*, 461 U.S. 138, 152 (1983). Therefore, it is incumbent on the agency's brass and internal affairs investigators not to disregard what most consider the most disruptive words spoken in an agency: rumors, gossip, grapevine, hearsay, etc.

Rumors

A typical scenario is where an officer peeks into a supervisor's office and feeds the supervisor some juicy gossip that is going around the police department involving at least one member of the agency. After the gossip is spilled, the sending officer tells the supervisor he does not want to be involved and what he spilt should be held in confidence. At this point, the officer departs, leaving the supervisor with nothing but hearsay and many times a leaky bag of aggravation and potential litigation depending on what the rumor is.

When a supervisor or internal affairs investigator hears a rumor on purpose or accidentally even if he does not believe at the time that it has the potential of being disruptive to the agency, it is his responsibility to address it swiftly but appropriately. (Many times the initial gossip a supervisor receives is taken as insignificant and of little or no value; however, just as many times this initially insignificant rumor turns out to be significant. Therefore, all rumors regardless of their initial value should be documented.) *Swiftly* is self-explanatory; *appropriately*, at minimum, should start by having (ordering if necessary) the gossiping officer document what he knows about the rumor and reminding the gossiping officer that whatever is provided will be held as confidential as the law allows. At this point, officers should be made to understand that while under the *First Amendment* the filing of grievances is generally considered constitutionally protected forms of speech, the mere filing of a complaint (e.g., spreading rumors) against another member of the agency, under Garcetti, would more than likely be considered a speech in accordance to their official duties; therefore, disciplinary action is not unthinkable or unrealistic but possible. See *Viola v. Borough of Throop*, 2010 U.S. App. LEXIS 15455 (3d Cir. Pa. July 22, 2010); *Houskins v. Sheahan*, 549 F. 3d 480, 7th Circuit (2008).

Blogs, Websites, and Forums

It seems that common sense, more often than not, takes a back seat when it is suspected an officer in the department anonymously posts on a blog, website, and/or forum from anywhere else but police headquarters. Unless the investigator can prove with one hundred percent certainty that the police officer was the physical person behind the computer and literally typing the keystrokes, the department's chance at sustaining a disciplinary charge is not impossible, but is certainly minimal.

All allegations, even anonymous posts dishonoring the police department or brass that administrators have reason to believe was authored by an officer, should tread lightly on drawing any preconceived conclusions without first a thorough, accurate, and complete investigation. At minimum, the posts should be printed, all witnesses should be interviewed, and the target officer(s) should be interviewed even if all the target officers deny being the author.

Specific words, comments, and details expressed in the blogs, websites, and forums may not be enough to accuse an officer of being the author, but they could be used to point the investigator in the direction of who inside the department released confidential or law enforcement sensitive material. To be clear, unless the officer confesses, the chances of knowing who specifically authored a post will be near to impossible even if the Internet Protocol Address is known. But if only isolated officers in the department possess unique classified information and it is this information that is posted, the investigator can narrow down the suspects. Under these situations the investigation into who wrote the post would take a back seat to the collateral investigation as to who released confidential records and/or information.

As broached in the preceding paragraphs, all target officers should be questioned on whether or not they either authored the post or know the identity of the person or persons who authored the post. Beforehand, especially in this type investigation, the internal affairs investigator should clearly inform the target officers they will be sworn to their statements *before* the first question is asked.

Social Networking

Keeping up with the current trends of the past couple years with regards to internal affairs investigations, it is only fitting to write a piece on social networking, considering there are many officers who create and use these type accounts (e.g., MySpace, Facebook, etc.).

Although officers have a right to maintain personal web pages, websites, and social networking accounts their status as a public official and officer in the police department requires that the content of those sites not be in violation of existing agency policy or directives; therefore, it is probably wise to have such a policy. *No policy* equals *No notice,* which means there will be an upward battle should charges be filed based on the Chief's arbitrary and capricious viewpoint that the content is objectionable.

For policy purposes, a good start would include, but not be limited to, the following:

- Officers' behavior both on and off duty is always subject to the rules and regulations of the police department and any such activity bringing discredit to the department is strictly pro-hibited.

- Any activity bringing discredit to the officer's status as a member of the department is strictly prohibited.

- Officers are prohibited from expressing personal opinions on matters related to the department or policies within.

- Items, objects, or material not supported under public domain and considered official agency property (e.g. photographs, statements, reports, etc.) shall not be used or displayed on any officer websites without the written consent of the Chief.

When a suspicious website is brought to the internal affairs investigator's attention, it is important that initially this information remains undisclosed to the target officer or anyone not on a need-to-know basis. Keeping these type investigations (e.g., forum posts, websites, etc.) initially secret until every single page on the site(s) are printed, archived, or stored for future reference is important to the case. If necessary, a third party computer consultant should be employed to capture any on-site videos, site sources, IP addresses, and so on. (With the frequency of computer type investigations going on across the country, having an on-call computer consultant is highly suggested.)

Once the pages are safely stored, then broached in blogs, websites, and forums, the internal affairs investigator will rely on the investigatory interview and truthfulness of the target officer to confirm or deny an alleged violation of the policies linked to the target. This sole reliance is necessary only if the site's words, pictures, and videos fail to provide ample supportive documentation to prove by the preponderance of all evidence collected that the target officer wasn't indirectly or directly involved in the site or material. This being the case, the target officer needs to be sworn to his statement and reminded of the consequences of false swearing. In spite of this, the investigator needs to remember that the probability of this type of investigation being sustained immediately, is rare. Unless and until the statute of limitations ends on criminal misconduct, the sworn statement denying knowledge remains a possibility to investigate criminally later, should new information come to light confirming that the officer lied. Hence, while the target officer's statement may not prove useful in departmental charges today, their sworn (preferably "White Sheet" handwritten words) statement if proven untruthful later may come back to haunt the officer far worse than any departmental charges.

Chapter 13
Incapacity: Unfit-for-Duty

There is only one question with three parts that a Chief needs to answer to determine whether an officer is fit or unfit for duty. Answering "yes" to any of these parts should heighten the chief's awareness regarding this officer, and it is suggested the officer should be sent to a medical professional to verify or negate the Chief's conclusions.

The Chief needs to ask: Is the officer ready, willing, and able to perform his official duties as assigned? Or, more accurately presented given the circumstances: Is the officer unready, unwilling, and/or unable to perform his official duties as assigned? At this point, answering "no" to any one (i.e., unready, unwilling, or unable), individually or any combination of the three, should be concerning to the Chief. The Chief should first define how the phrase "perform his official duties as assigned" applies to his department. As much as every agency is similar in many law enforcement aspects, they are just as dissimilar in internal policies and procedures including, but not limited to, an officer's duties.

Determining whether an officer can *perform his official duties as assigned*, as it relates to whether an officer is fit-for-duty, should begin before the officer is hired and again every time the officer receives a promotion. If the agency did not address an officer's official duties when first hired or readdressed them when promoted, it is not too late to take steps now to put together the supportive documentation that could be presented in an incapacity hearing in support of the Chief's position.

In preparation of an incoming recruit, the chief should extract the section of the law, rules, or policies that lists the specific *responsibilities* of a police officer. Each individual responsibility needs to be listed separately on a sheet of paper preceding a line long enough for the officer to insert his initials and the date (see Appendix B). While the sample is not inclusive, it is recommended that every department create a checklist that mirrors the actual duties and responsibilities of the officers within their agency. Either before, during, or immediately after the interview, but before the promissory of employment, the Chief should provide the applicants with a copy of the "Police Officer Responsibilities" checklist. This same process should be done for anyone seeking promotion, but obviously with the checklist for the specific rank applied for.

The applicant (or candidate if a promotion) should take the check-list and be directed to review each and every responsibility within the next seventy-two hours, and he would be instructed to initial and date in blue ink (to prove originality) only those responsibilities the applicant is able to perform if and when assigned. The Chief needs to explain, up front, to the applicant that the responsibilities listed are those that are expected to be repeatedly performed by all police officers in the department, and unless required by law no accommodations would be provided under any circumstances. The applicant should be told to return the checklist only if he is ready, willing, and able to perform the responsibilities.

Once returned, this checklist will:

(1) Fortify the applicant's confirmation that he is ready, willing, and able to perform the official duties if and when assigned, or

(2) Confirm the applicant is unready, unwilling, or unable to perform the official duties as assigned.

Obviously, if the outcome is the latter, the applicant/candidate will not be hired by the department or eligible for promotion. On the other hand, if the applicant confirms through his initials his readiness, ability, and willingness to perform the official duties as assigned, then the applicant/candidate successfully satisfied, at least, this crucial prerequisite. By satisfying this prerequisite voluntarily and without pressure, the applicant has personally reinforced his abilities, medically and physically, to perform the required tasks of the agency.

Once returned, and if the applicant is hired or promoted, the completed checklist in most cases will remain dormant in an officer's personnel file untouched throughout their distinguished police career. That is, unless and until it comes to the Chief's attention that the officer may not be able to perform his duties as assigned.

Reasonable Cause

The *Equal Employment Opportunity Commission* has defined a "Medical Examination" as "a procedure or test that seeks information about an individual's physical or mental impairments or health"[25] stating "an examination which reflects whether applicants have characteristics that lead to identifying whether the individual has excessive anxiety, depression, and certain compulsive disorders ... [are]

---

[25] ADA Enforcement Guidance: Preemployment Disability-Related Questions and Medical Examinations (1995).

medical." *Id.* On the other hand, "if a test is designed and used to measure only things such as honesty, tastes, and habits, it is not medical." *Id.* To determine if a law enforcement officer is physically conditioned to perform the duties as assigned, such examination is medical. Obviously non-medical tests (e.g., "statement analysis") can be handled by qualified police officers, but medical tests can be conducted only by medical professionals. Therefore, things that may warrant a fit for duty exam include, but are not limited to, a change in the officer's performance, excessive use of sick leave, poor performance or judgment, illnesses, injuries (on the job and off), allegations of excessive force, and peculiar behavior.

Regardless of the reasonable cause that leads the Chief or internal affairs investigator to conclude a fitness for duty examination is needed, the investigator needs to document the facts that have led them to that conclusion. Third person complaints need to be documented to the investigator if applicable by the third person in their own handwriting and in their own words. The investigator should not summarize a third person's complaint unless all other avenues are exhausted or unavailable. If the third person complainant is an agency officer, they should be ordered to give their account if not done voluntarily. These facts should be in chronological order and specify the date, time, location, and the events as they unfolded. Anything and everything related to this investigation is to be confidential and should be released only under lawful circumstances.

Once it is determined the officer will be going to a department's doctor, the officer should be summarily informed of the reason behind the referral with vague enough information to not place the officer on the defensive, but with enough information to give him a general over-sight into the department's concern. During this discussion, the internal affairs investigator should notify the officer there is a zero tolerance for lying or being deceptive to the doctor and anything less than the absolute truth should not be accepted, encouraged, or tolerated with the Chief treating the lie as a terminable offense.

Once notified, the officer then has two choices: (1) voluntarily submit to the professional evaluation or (2) voluntarily refuse to submit to the professional evaluation. If he refuses, it is possible a sustained violation could lead to a termination of his services. However, if he refuses to waive his rights to privacy concerns based on HIPPA or ADA laws or his right to hold harmless the professional examiner, the department's legal advisor may need to determine whether the police department will accept the liability of the medical professional to have the examination completed. Regarding his privacy rights, it is not uncommon now for the officer to authorize the release of the findings and recommendations, but not the report. Considering that to the police department the findings and recommendations are what is important for their investigation, this demand normally goes unchallenged. Another item worth resolving before examination is who specifically receives the outcome and who is permitted to read it beyond the chief of police and/or internal affairs investigators.

The officer should be notified through an established policy, but reminded verbally by the internal affairs investigator, that his attendance at the appointment should be without his lawyer, union representative, and firearm. A family member or friend may be the exception if a ride is needed to and from the appointment, but that person's role is limited to the ride. The officer should be instructed to bring with him any and all medical reports and medical equipment (e.g., glasses, diabetic device, etc.) that will be necessary for the doctor to make a fair and reasonable medical evaluation.

Once it comes to the Chief's attention that an officer may be in need of some medical or psychological attention, it is incumbent on the internal affairs investigators to immediately take action. If the reason is psychological, the officer's firearm should be secured as soon as possible by an on-duty supervisor or better yet an internal affairs investigator. Obviously, there should be no delay in retrieving the weapon, but the officer should be reassured that the taking of his firearm is for the protection of himself and others. The officer should be placed on suspension with pay and sent home; however, he should already know from existing policy, but reminded verbally by internal affairs, that the immediate action taken is not considered discipline or punishment and at this time his badge and identification would not be confiscated. An appointment should be made as quickly as possible with a police psychologist (i.e., Ph.D.) or psychiatrist (M.D.). The officer should be informed of the scheduled appointment in writing and an acknowledgment should be confirmed by him. If necessary, the internal affairs investigator should take steps to assist him in getting to and from the appointment if a family member or friend is not available. If the reason is medical (e.g., illness or injury) the firearm may be retrieved depending on the extent of the injury. If the injury is to his strong hand, arm, or prevents him from firing his weapon for whatever reason, his weapon should be retrieved; otherwise, taking a firearm would be considered on a case-by-case basis. Unlike psychological where a suspension with pay would be in the officer's best interest, if the department can reassign the injured officer it should be examined again on a case-by-case basis. Obviously, if the injury or illness (e.g., contagious illnesses) prevents an officer from being assigned restricted duty, a non-disciplinary suspension with pay (aka: Administrative Leave) should be implemented. Like psychological, the internal affairs investigators should make the initial appointment with the department's physician, confirm notification in writing with the officer, and make arrangements if necessary to assist him in getting to the appointment. However, to be clear, attendance is his responsibility and not that of the agency or the agency's representatives.

Now that the officer is being sent to the police department's physician or psychologist, the checklist will be a useful tool to determine the officer's level of fitness as well as clarify what work-related restrictions (e.g., light duty assignments) the officer can and cannot do. That is, the police department's medical doctor or psychologist would be given a copy of the identical responsibilities checklist the applicant received before he was hired. The checklist lines would be blank and the doctor(s) would be pre-instructed to check only those responsibilities the officer is able to perform in relationship to his injury and/or illness. This completed checklist would not replace, but would be in addition to, the doctor's findings and recommendations they normally provide.

Once the checklist and recommendations are received from the doctor, the internal affairs investigator should immediately verify that the doctor's unchecked responsibilities match the doctor's recommendations. In other words, the doctor's recommendations on how the officer is going to fully recover should correspond with the unchecked responsibilities to guarantee that once the officer satisfies all of the doctor's recommendations then at the same time all the unchecked responsibilities will be satisfied, and he once again will be fit for duty. If there are unchecked responsibilities not consistent with the doctor recommendations, the internal affairs investigator needs to contact the doctor to either receive additional recommendations or have the checklist updated so both are consistent.

Putting aside the various reasons as to why an officer could be unable, unwilling, and unready to perform the duties they were hired for, the internal affairs investigator, after seeing the medical professional's recommendation and checklist, should send a letter by regular and certified mail to the officer giving him five calendar days to provide the steps he needs to take to fully satisfy the doctor's recommendations. The chances are strong that once the officer receives the letter by regular mail, he will not accept delivery of the certified letter and it will be returned undelivered. When this happens, the investigator should not open the envelope. The envelope will be opened by either the hearing officer or court should charges be filed and confirmation is needed to prove (1) the letter was sent and (2) the content of the letter. This letter will place the obligation on the officer to tell the department what he will do to satisfy the recommendations as opposed to what the department will order him to do; thus, avoiding a claim by the officer or his attorney that the demands are unreasonable.

Once the officer receives the order he has two options: comply or not. The chances of him complying personally are far and few between, however, he will probably send the letter to his attorney seeking a legal opinion. For the officer's sake, his attorney would need to react within the five-day window or if no response is provided on or before the fifth day, internal affairs would immediately open an investigation against the officer for insubordination (i.e., failure and/or refusal to follow the direct order). At this time and under these circumstances, the suspension would continue and he would be interviewed regarding his noncompliance. When this happens, chances are good that the officer will fall back on his attorney in defense of his noncompliance; however, he would be reminded through the interview process that his attorney does not run the police department, the Chief of Police does. Interestingly, the fit-for-duty examination becomes secondary now to the insubordination charge and his fitness for duty may not even be an issue any longer because insubordination is a terminable offense.

Anyhow, if he complies with the letter's order and provides his recommendations, the internal affairs investigator needs to check with the doctor to make certain the steps he provided will indeed accomplish the goal and will be appropriate for the recommendations the doctor presented. If so, the officer would be advised in writing that the steps he gave were acceptable to both the doctor and the Chief. Once the officer completes the steps, the decision as to whether or not a reevaluation is needed would be left up to the doctor. Furthermore, because the checklist would obviously have at least one blank line representing her inability to perform at least one job function he verified he was able to do when hired, he will have to be reassigned to restricted duty, reassigned outside the police department, take accrued time, or go unpaid until the steps are complete.

If, for whatever reason, the officer does not comply with the steps he presented and the police department and doctor agreed with, he should again be investigated for insubordination, and also now for him being unfit-for-duty (i.e., until he completes the recommendations, his fitness for duty is pending). Other than the doctor's report, the officer's presented steps to recovery, the letters exchanged, and the officer's investigatory interview, the pre-hiring checklist will also be treated as evidence to support an incapacity charge.

With very limited valid reasons for noncompliance, his days with the police department are all but numbered. Once the investigation is complete, internal affairs should turn the entire report over to the Chief who, after finding sufficient information to file charges, will, in all likelihood, file accordingly. From here it's in the hands of the hearing officer who will ultimately determine the disposition of the charges and a fitting penalty (e.g., termination).

Even if a valid reason was offered for his noncompliance, the fact remains that he continues to be unfit for duty. This being the case, the Chief would still be filing charges against the officer, but leaving out the insubordination count. Once the officer receives the preliminary notice of discipline he will seek a medical or psychological opinion from his own doctor if this was not already done when he received the recommendations letter. If his own doctor determines he is unfit for duty he may go for another opinion, but the chances are slim that the internal affairs investigator or department will ever find out about his first opinion even if the matter goes to a hearing. On the other hand, regardless of what doctor he finds to evaluate his condition, he will not possess the supportive documentation leading up to the need for the department's initial examination or any of the department's records; therefore, the investigator and Chief should not be surprised if his doctor clears him and finds no medical conditions that would preempt him from full active duty.

Because the charges are already filed and the hearing is forthcoming, it is predictable his doctor's report, at minimum, will be a material fact he will present to counter the department's doctor. However, because his doctor had limited information to go by before he rendered his decision, a disclaimer may be in his findings indicating his information is based solely on the records in his possession and additional records or information may modify the findings accordingly. (This disclaimer is an important line the prosecutor will use in a hearing to question the validity of his doctor's findings; therefore, it should be highlighted.)

Interestingly, whether the officer is fit or not could be decided more on the checklist comparisons (i.e., pre-hired checklist versus fit-for-duty checklist), because if the officer is unready and unable to perform the identical job duties he was able and ready to perform when he was first hired, he understood, and he accepted, then his means of defense will be severely affected. More so, when the department put him on notice that except by law no accommodations will be provided, he will have a difficult, if not impossible, time being granted a reassignment.

In all too many cases, compassion stops the Chief from filing departmental charges against the police officer even when evidence is overwhelming that the officer is unfit for duty. In the department's best interest, the Chief should file the appropriate charges against the officer immediately on having sufficient information to do so. The hearing can always be waived by the Chief should it later be determined to be in the department's best interest to not move in that direction at that time (e.g., attorneys working on settlement agreement), but this should be done only after the officer has been served. Another option generally put on the table by the impartial hearing officer is a third binding examination by a doctor mutually agreed on by all parties. If the parties cannot come to a mutual selection, the hearing officer would give them three doctors to choose from, and if they cannot mutually agree on one of the three then the hearing officer would just select one, but the hearing officer making the selection should be the very last option. With the third doctor's decision being binding, if found to be fit for duty like the officer's doctor claims, the department will possess two doctors' opinions and would return the officer to duty. Conversely, if the third doctor's medical opinion is that the officer continues to be unfit for duty, he will be permanently relieved of duty.

Incontrovertibly when the Chief is facing an officer who is confirmed medically and/or psychologically incapacitated and who can no longer perform the job responsibilities of the position he was initially hired to do, termination is the only practical resolution. However logical and practical termination may be under those circumstances, termination is not the best choice and should be left as a last resort only. A problem with terminating an officer under these circumstances, which departments have discovered years later, is if and when the officer fully satisfies the recommendations of the police department's doctor and is now fit for duty (i.e., can perform all the responsibilities on the checklist), he may be returned to active duty. Although atypical, it is a factor the Chief has to take into consideration when dealing with these types of cases; therefore, depending on the facts and circumstances, asking for and receiving a resignation letter is recommended.

Chapter 14
Workplace Privacy

The right of the people to be secure in their persons, houses, papers and effects, against unreasonable searches and seizures, shall not be violated, and no warrants shall issue, but upon probable cause, supported by oath or affirmation, and particularly describing the place to be searched, and the persons or things to be seized. **U.S. Constitution, Amendment IV**

There are two fundamental types of workplace searches:

(1) Workplace searches where the investigator is searching for evidence connected to a criminal allegation.

(2) Workplace searches where the investigator is searching for something related to the officer's employ (e.g., evidence related to a departmental investigation or non-investigatory search).

When conducting a criminal investigation involving a police officer, stop, do not pass go, and confirm first that a search warrant is not needed before taking any action. If you are unsure, than DO NOTHING until the advice of a competent management's labor attorney is received.

What if the internal affairs investigator's investigation does not rise to criminal misconduct and is limited to only policy violations: Does a police officer have a reasonable expectation of privacy in their offices, desks, computers, and filing cabinets? What standards must a supervisor follow to lawfully conduct a warrantless search of those areas? Must a supervisor have probable cause to search a government employee's workplace? All these questions and many more first need to be resolved by the investigator before he even thinks about opening an officer's locker or desk drawer.

Absent an allegation or investigation, it is not unthinkable and quite common for a police supervisor or even a co-worker to retrieve an active citizen's investigation off of a detective's desk, borrow a fellow officer's piece of equipment from their lockers, or use each other's desk phones, computers, typewriters, or fax machines. This camaraderie sharing, for the most part, is necessary for an efficient and effective police operation when proactive officers are involved. However, even when relaxed teamwork is commonplace, an officer's privacy rights cannot be taken for granted by an internal affairs investigator, and the target officer's rights still need to be carefully measured.

For this reason, before the investigator takes on an investigation in the workplace, it is important he knows that a workplace is an area generally under the control of the employer (e.g., offices, desks, filing cabinets, computers, and government vehicles) but is used by the officer due to the employer / employee relationship. See *O'Connor v. Ortega*, 480 US 709, 715 (1987) ("The workplace includes those areas and items that are related to work and are generally within the employer's control"). And while in *O'Connor* "the hallways, cafeteria, offices, desks, and file cabinets, among other areas, are all part of the [hospital] workplace" *Id.* at 716, it would not be unreasonable to draw the assumption that a police department's workplace environment would not be too dissimilar. Additionally, the courts have held that "government supervisor may inspect work area of subordinate to evaluate his job performance," *United States v. Kahan*, 350 F.Supp. 784, 793 (S.D.N.Y.1972) (dictum), *rev'd on other grounds*, 479 F.2d 290 (2d Cir.1973), *rev'd per curiam*, 415 U.S. 293, 94 (1974); therefore, leaving the impression as long as the inspection is not unreasonably applied (i.e., inspection is not purpose driven), the work area is accessible. Furthermore, "if there are reasonable grounds to believe that the search will uncover evidence of the employee's misconduct, the search is justified at its inception." *Ortega*, 480 U.S. at 726, 107 S.Ct. at 1502; *Shields*, 874 F.2d at 1202 quoting *Gossmeyer v. McDonald*, 128 F.3d 481, 494 (7th Cir. 1997). The workplace and area under the Chief's control differs greatly from an officer's personal effects which are only for the moment, located at the employer's place of business, but at the same time remain the property of the officer (e.g., handbag, briefcase, jacket). The officer is notified that his personal property, which is located at the employer's place of business, is susceptible to a search or the officer uses his personal property for work purposes. An example of an officer's personal property that could be susceptible to a search would be her personal cellular telephone (see below), during those times when he uses it while on duty.

An investigator's obligation to recognize an officer's personal property cannot be understated or mistakenly labeled. When a target officer brings her handbag into work every day, and it is known it serves as a vehicle to store her car keys, wallet, and other personal items, it is not open to inspection and anything retrieved from the handbag without a search warrant will likely violate the officer's constitutional Fourth Amendment rights. As a result, the internal affairs investigator needs to determine first and foremost how the property attaches to the police department, why it is there, and who brought it. If in the end it is concluded the property is unquestionably the officer's personal property, attached to the department only temporarily with an isolated and justifiable purpose, a search warrant should be secured. More so, if the investigator has any doubt, any second thoughts, or any hesitation in determining connection between the property under question and the search or seizure as it relates to the necessity to secure a search warrant—a search warrant should be secured. Nonetheless, any and all searches should be done so cautiously so as not to reveal the employee's personal items not related to her workplace setting as to prevent any tortuous invasion of her privacy rights. See *K-Mart Corp. Store No. 7441 v. Trotti,* 677 S.W.2d 632 (Tex. App.1984).

Waiver

In accepting a public position, police officers may have watereddown expectations of privacy when related to the job. But with different departments having Chiefs with different philosophies and various policies, the level of an officer's reasonable expectation of privacy has to be considered on an agency-by-agency basis. Accepting workplace privacy rights are not absolute and are reviewed on a case-by-case basis; therefore, over the years many Chiefs have adopted or introduced some form of regulation in heeding the advice of the courts.

Accordingly, for the investigator there are several places he should look to determine if any workplace privacy rights have been waived by the target officer. These waivers, if nothing else, indisputably put the officer on notice that he might be required at one time or another to submit to a search by the Chief or his designee. This waiver could have been by direct (e.g., signed something) or indirect (e.g., policy) means; therefore, the investigator should start by going through the employee personnel manual to see if there are any phrases like, "at all times police officers are subject to examination and inspection by duly authorized officials in the discharge of their official duties." Other documents that may have inserted waivers include the officers' collective bargaining agreement, which could authorize random inspections and a department policy that would spell out monitoring or searches that can greatly diminish an officer's expectation of privacy depending upon what is written. Additionally, many Chiefs require newly appointed rookies to read and sign a waiver similar to the sample that follows.

WAIVER

The DEPARTMENT NAME may assign to its members and employees departmentally owned vehicles, lockers, keys, desks, cabinets, computers, phones, et cetera for the mutual convenience of the department and its personnel. Such equipment is and remains the property of the DEPARTMENT NAME. Personnel are reminded that storage of personal items in, on or attached to borough property is at the employee's own risk and is subject to entry, inspection, and monitoring without notice.

If none of these waiver stipulations are in effect in the police department, it is certainly in the internal affairs investigator's best interest with regards to future departmental investigations to circulate a similar waiver like the above to every single member under the Chief's chain of command. This waiver should be hand delivered, reviewed, and signed accordingly.

Regardless of which waiver the department has in place, it is important to have, at least, one procedure as *O'Connor* opined, "[p]ublic employees' expectations of privacy in their offices, desks, and file cabinets, like similar expectations of employees in the private sector, may be reduced by virtue of actual office practices and procedures, or by legitimate regulation." *Id.* at 717. Absent any "legitimate regulation" could obviously put the Chief and internal affairs investigator in a position of determining an officer's level of privacy on an arbitrary and capricious basis; thus, giving greater opportunity for any target officer's attorney to challenge their decision and the search.

Another waiver Chiefs across the country should separately implement is a private cellular telephone usage waiver (see sample below) for those officers who voluntarily choose to use their own cellular telephones while on-duty. The waiver is used to get limitless access to an officer's itemized phone records (i.e., calls, texts) during an officer's on-duty hours should the need arise.

CELL PHONE WAIVER

Officers who use their private cellular telephone while on-duty shall provide the Chief, internal affairs unit, or designees, upon request, a copy of his/her detailed monthly cellular telephone bill covering periods of time the employee is on-duty.

The cases that follow, out of thousands of examples on point, show the importance behind a Chief maintaining an effective regulation:

◇ *United States v. Simons*, 206 F.3d 392, 398 (4th Cir. 2000), which held "that the remote searches of [the employee's] computer did not violate his Fourth Amendment rights because, in light of the Internet policy, [the employee] lacked a legitimate expectation of privacy in the files downloaded from the Internet. Additionally, [they] conclude[d] that [the employee's] Fourth Amendment rights were not violated by [Foreign Bureau of Information Services] retrieval of Simons' hard drive from his office."

◇ *American Postal Workers Union v. United States Postal Service*, 871 F.2d 556, 560 (6th Cir. 1989) held "The Fourth Amendment right to a reasonable search can, however, be waived. The employees hired after 1973 expressly waived their rights under the Fourth Amendment when they signed Postal Service Form 4943, which reads in part … "Locker is subject to inspection at any time by authorized personnel." All of the named plaintiffs in the instant case signed the 1973 version of the form.

◇ *Simmons v. Southwestern Bell Tel. Co.*, 452 F.Supp. 392, 396 (W.D.Okla.1978) *aff'd*, 611 F.2d 342 (10th Cir. 1979) opined, "plaintiff knew his calls were monitored, he had no reasonable expectation that his calls would remain private."

◇ *O'Connor v. Ortega*, 480 US 709 (1987) held "there are reasonable grounds for suspecting that the search will turn up evidence that the employee is guilty of work related mis-conduct, or that the search is necessary for a noninvestigative work-related purpose such as to retrieve a needed file."

◇ *New Jersey v. T.L.O.*, 469 U.S. 325, 342 (1985) held "a search will be permissible in its scope when the measures adopted are reasonably related to the objectives of the search and not excessively intrusive."

◇ *United States v. Bunkers*, 521 F.2d 1217, 1221 (9th Cir. 1975) held "that Bunkers' voluntary entrance into postal service employment and his acceptance and use of the locker subject to the regulatory leave of inspection and search and the labor union's contractual rights of search upon reasonable suspicion of criminal activity amount to an effective relinquishment of Bunkers' Fourth Amendment immunity in his work connected use of the locker."

Contrary to these examples, given the importance of maintaining a practice and procedure that allows for the search of department owned and officer's use of property, it is understandable when searches are undertaken *without regulation* the courts take a closer look. An example of this out of the 3rd Circuit happened when the court concluded "there is no regulation and no police practice ... which would alert an officer to expect unconsented locker searches[; therefore, the officer] met his burden of showing a constitutionally justified expectation of privacy in his locker." *United States v. Speights*, 557 F.2d 362, 363 (3d Cir. 1977) held that "a privacy interest in an office reserved for one's exclusive use at a place of employment to be reasonable, especially when asserted against a forcible entry after work hours," *United States v. Taketa*, 923 F.2d 665, 669 (9th Cir. 1991). Acknowledging a Fourth Amendment right may exist regarding an internal affairs investigator's authority to involuntarily search and seize property, even if the property belongs to the department, the court in *O'Connor* offered some guidance in "[d]etermining the reasonableness of any search" *supra @ 726* by giving a twofold inquiry the investigator would use:

(1) From the onset, was the search justified? In other words, did the officer possess an actual expectation before the search took place that the area in question was secured from unreasonable searches and seizures? More so, would a reasonable and prudent person in an identical situation accept that the area searched was reasonable, because maybe the officer waived his privacy expectation or there is a clause in his collective bargaining agreement, the personnel manual, or a specific policy that would have lowered his expectation? If not directly or indirectly put on notice, was the area in question open and unrestricted to other officers or was the area secured with access limited to the officer? Was the desk, cabinet, locker, and et cetera accessible through a department's master key or key distributed by the department, or are officers permitted to use their own lock? Are the computer and files password protected and, if so, is the password distributed by the department and

kept on file for unannounced monitoring or did the officer set his own password(s) and was never obligated to provide the password(s) to his supervisors? Is the property in question the personal property of the officer, which is temporarily brought to the workplace for rational reasons (e.g., winter coat worn to work in the winter and put in locker during shift)?

Obviously, these points briefly provide some examples of questions the internal affairs investigator should resolve before carrying out any search. To not take the possibility of losing whatever items are collected, it should be strongly considered to discuss the circumstances with a competent management labor attorney. However, if it is determined the area or property to be searched or seized cannot be justified given the circumstances and facts presented to the investigator, the search or seizure should not move forward and there would be no reason to even consider the second part of the inquiry. On the other hand, if the search or seizure is conclusively determined from the onset to be justified, then,

(2) The investigator must be assured, with no hesitation, that the area to be searched and the property to be seized is reasonable when compared to the facts and circumstances specific to the allegations before him. That is, for example, if the allegation surrounds a missing shotgun, a search of the officer's desk drawers on the surface would be unjustified, unless there is reason to believe the weapon was dismantled. On the other hand, searching an officer's vertical six-foot locker would not be unthinkable if and when item number one has been resolved to the investigator's satisfaction.

At any time or for any reason the internal affairs investigator does not believe with 100 percent certainty that he has satisfied both parts it goes without writing, no search should take place. However, if and when a search does take place, the investigator should, at minimum, take pictures of the area in question before the search and all those items collected during the search. If a videocamera is available that would be beneficial, because a picture tells a thousand words. Before the search, on tape, the investigator can document the reason behind the need to search and how they came to the conclusion a search is reasonable in the specific areas in question. Also, the investigator should record who is in the room while the search is being conducted and, in adhering to the chain of custody, all evidence should be lodged according to policy and procedure.

Chapter 15
Absenteeism

According to a *CareerBuilder*™ survey,[26] 32 percent of workers admitted to calling in sick with fake excuses. Thirty-two out of one-hundred employees who likely concluded they were *entitled to* or *earned* the day off even though they were not sick. And while the causes for employees to take off are related to legitimate reasons like their own health problems or the health problems of one of their dependents, they take advantage by using sick time for:

(1) Personal responsibilities;

(2) Poor attitudes;

(3) Their dissatisfaction with the job;

(4) Lack of management oversight, etc.

Obviously, an officer using a sick day for anything other than being sick or caring for a dependent should not be tolerated by the Chief and should be swiftly investigated by the internal affairs investigator.

Interestingly, one of the most common barriers to decreasing absenteeism is supervisor resistance even when police unions and the officer's resistance are low. That is, most supervisors (e.g., sergeants) are hesitant to address an officer's absence directly with an officer even when the union officials and co-workers expect some type of recourse. To put the union's acceptance in perspective, it is an on-duty officer (i.e., union member) who gets inconveniently held over to cover for an absent officer's shift; thus, placing the union between the member who is abusing his sick time versus the member who has to cover the open shift. Placing the union in this conflicting position frequently, but covertly, calls for some type of administrative action. Management's failure to react to sick day usage that is causing a problem in the agency could lead to unscrupulous officers excessively abusing their sick time benefits; therefore, every sick day taken should be reviewed.

Police departments across the country have instituted various programs to address absenteeism problems like paid leave banks, buyback programs, bonuses, no fault days, personal recognition, and

---

[26] http://www.careerbuilder.com/share/aboutus/pressreleasesdetail.aspx?id=pr336&sd=11%2F27%2F2006&ed=12%2F31%2F2006

clauses where officers are given a certain number of unexcused or unexplained absences (e.g., mental health day). Even with these types of programs in place there will be officers who continue to take advantage of the system. Accordingly, the Chief needs to institute an all-inclusive absenteeism policy and actively discipline those officers who are violating it. More important than the implementation of an absenteeism policy in many respects is a Verification of Illness form (see Appendix C). A policy without a verification form the officer needs to sign that verifies their absence was legitimate will not be as effective. It is this form which, if signed under false pretenses, could serve as evidence toward criminal charges, that will conscientiously stop borderline officers from fraudulently being absent.

First and foremost, the internal affairs investigator needs to under-stand that absenteeism is not limited to just an officer calling in sick. This is important because an officer can be out on bereavement for a loved one who is still alive or feigns a 60-day injury every July with Doctor Summeroff. Therefore, absenteeism is defined as an occurrence when an officer is away from their assigned tour of duty with or with-out permission. Absenteeism includes, but is not limited to, leaving early, showing up late, sickness, disability, and being out due to workmen's compensation. Demanding a doctor's note is a useful admin-istrative tool to assist in compliance, but it should have no bearing on the investigator's objective in calculating abuse or excessiveness.

To accuse an officer of abuse or excessiveness, the investigator needs to fall back on the policy to assure the grounds are in place to warrant any charges. This is necessary because any charges based on less will be challenged successfully by the charged officer's competent defense attorney as arbitrary and capricious. To support the attorney's defense during a hearing, he will ask several sequestered officers in your department, including the Chief and if available a rookie, to define "abuse" and how many absences would be considered excessive. Without a policy, the answers will be inconsistent; thus, warranting the dismissal of any departmental charges. Within the agency's policy there should be an absolutely consistent answer to such questions using the terms "abuse" and "excessive" regardless of whom in the agency is defining it. A well-written and established policy is the only way to ensure this will happen.

General Diagnosis

Bewilderingly, Chiefs continue to place a lot of curious emphasis on ordering officers to produce doctors' notes that disclose the reason why the officer was out sick (i.e., general diagnosis) even if there is no legitimate business necessity to receive the diagnosis. Left unresolved and open to further challenge is what constitutes a business necessity, but it would appear that when a business necessity does not exist then "requiring a general diagnosis is sufficient to trigger the protections of the ADA," *Conroy v. New York State Dep't of Correctional Services*, 333 F.3d 88, 95 (2d Cir. 2003). Additionally, another court found that it would prohibit an employer from seeking the prescription drugs an employee was using because it may reveal an employee's disability. *Roe v. Cheyenne Mountain Conference Resort*, 920 F. Supp. 1153, 1154-55 (D. Colo. 1996), *aff'd in pertinent part*, 124 F.3d 1221 (10th Cir. 1997). For further guidance on this as stated, in part, under the United States Code on discrimination:

> *[The employer] shall not require a medical examination and shall not make inquiries of an employee as to whether such employee is an individual with a disability or as to the nature or severity of the disability, unless such examination or inquiry is shown to be **job-related** and consistent with business necessity (emphasis added), and*

> *[The employer] may conduct voluntary medical examinations, including voluntary medical histories, which are part of an employee health program available to employees at that work site. A covered entity may make inquiries into the ability of an employee to perform job-related functions. 42 U.S.C. § 12112(d)(4)(A)*

Federal regulations implementing the ADA provide similar protections. 29 C.F.R. 1630.13(b); 1630.14(c). The appendix to 29 C.F.R. 1630.13(b) explains that ... the purpose of this provision is to prevent the administration to employees of medical tests or inquiries that do not serve a legitimate business purpose. For example, if an employee suddenly starts to use increased amounts of sick leave or starts to appear sickly, an employer could not require that employee to be tested for AIDS, HIV infection, or cancer unless the employer can demonstrate that such testing is job-related and consistent with the business necessity. See *Senate Report* at 39; *House Labor Report* at 75; *House*

Judiciary Report at 44 quoting Section 1630.13(b) Code of Federal Regulations, Title 29, Labor, Pt. 900-1899, *Revised* as of July 1, 2009.

Given the above, if and when a reasonable suspicion exists that leads the Chief and/or internal affairs investigator to believe an officer's absence is job-related or consistent with a business necessity, a legal review may be needed with a competent management's labor attorney before compelling an officer to produce a general diagnosis. Better yet, sending an officer to the police department's medical professional, especially since neither the Chief nor the internal affairs investigator are qualified to medically interpret the Doctor's notes, which would limit any challenge a target officer may ponder.

Before an internal affairs investigator asks for a doctor's note that includes a general diagnosis or the names of those prescriptions an officer is taking, the investigator should first figure out what he's planning on doing with the information once it is received. If, for example, all he is going to do is turn it over to the department's medical doctor then maybe the best first step to take is just to send the officer to the department's doctor and eliminate the messenger.

Even though asking for a general diagnosis is frowned on, except under limited circumstances (i.e., business necessity), the verification of illness should still have a line available for the reason an officer proffers for being out sick. That is, when an officer calls and voluntarily shares with the supervisor the reason why they are calling out, the supervisor should put in quotes the officer's reason (e.g., "sore throat"). Although many times the officer spontaneously gives a reason innocently, there are times when the officer gives the reason on purpose (e.g., "stress," "chest pain," "back injury," etc.), and the supervisor needs to immediately bring those possible business necessity concerns to the internal affairs commander's attention.

Policy Must Haves

Apart from the boiler plate, absenteeism policies should include no less than the following: reporting conditions; telephone and home visit verifications; confinement requirements with exemptions; absence report; number of absences that automatically triggers a return to duty doctor's notes; and numerous applicable definitions (e.g., absence, pattern, occurrence, standard, etc.).

Unreasonable Application

While the police department controls if and when discipline will come off of an officer who failed and/or refused to follow the absenteeism policy, it is certain that any unreasonable application of the policy will be challenged. Therefore, as part of the internal affairs investigator's inquiry, he needs to be cognizant of not only what the target officer did or did not do, but also what direction was given and what steps were taken by the officer's supervisor. (Again, the supervisor's actions and/or inactions may warrant a collateral investigation.)

An absenteeism policy, like all policies, should not be so unreasonably applied that it unduly interferes with an officer's welfare or is employed in a manner that discriminates or harasses the officer. For example, if the policy permits home visitations or telephone verifications but is used for any other purpose, it should be of no surprise that in doing so it could amount to an egregious and inexcusable violation of the officer's privacy rights. Knowing the possibility exists for supervisor abuse, favoritism, or discrimination, an investigator would evaluate whether the phone calls or home visits went beyond the policies intent, which served as contributing circumstances behind the officer's insubordination.

Investigation

For investigatory purposes, the *only* issues for the investigator are:

(1) Suspected acts of insubordination (e.g., did the officer follow the policy or order as directed);

(2) Whether or not the officer can duly perform the expected job functions (e.g., is he unfit-for-duty); and

(3) Is the absence legitimate.

When conducting the investigation and finally writing the report, the investigator needs to include the total costs associated with the officer's absence. This should be part of the report with use of a spreadsheet listing expenses like the officer's salary paid on the day the officer was absent, the overtime amount to cover the officer's absence, and the costs to conduct the investigation.

Chapter 16
Dishonesty

Police officers who, without doubt, knowingly and purposefully take evasive actions to directly or indirectly deceive the honor of their profession by hiding the truth from their superiors or society have done so knowing they have in all probability solidified their future. Being an ethical, honest, and honorable law enforcement officer is a fundamental prerequisite for being a police officer and the only acceptable and justified penalty for any irreversible sworn employee's unthinkable behavior of dishonesty is termination. A dishonest officer is a liability to a police department and whatever steps are necessary to remove a dishonest officer from the department should be employed. However, there is a thick line between a law enforcement officer accused of dishonesty and an officer who is actually dishonest; therefore, just because a target officer is accused of or receives charges of untruthfulness does not mean the officer is dishonest. To be clear, it is not until after a sustained finding on a specific violation of untruthfulness that there is the appropriate outcome of termination for the officer.

Those agencies that opt not to terminate an officer after he, in his official capacity, lied or filed a false police report, need to take a close look at some key decisions rendered by our courts since the early sixties that call into question the credibility of any future courtroom testimony of the officer who lied. Additionally and probably more concerning for the agency and taxpayers are various court decisions that held that police officers are obligated to disclose any exculpatory evidence favorable to the defense and if this disclosure is not done they may be civilly liable for the deprivation of the rights of the defendant. Specifically, 42 U.S.C. § 1983, which states in part:

> Every person who, under color of any statute, ordinance, regulation, custom, or usage, of any State or Territory or the District of Columbia, subjects, or causes to be subjected, any citizen of the United States or other person within the jurisdiction thereof to the deprivation of any rights, privileges, or immunities secured by the Constitution and laws, shall be liable to the party injured in an action at law, suit in equity, or other proper proceeding for redress.

Keeping an officer in the department who has been found guilty of untruthfulness demands the never-ending requirement that the officer disclose to the prosecutor(s) his personnel file and the fact that his count for lying was sustained. Such a disclosure would most certainly be used by the defense to successfully impeach the officer's credibility at trial with an acquittal as the possible outcome; if knowingly non-disclosed there is a high probability a civil suit will follow.

The courts have held that while "the ultimate duty of disclosure on the prosecutor, it would be anomalous to say that police officers are not liable when they affirmatively conceal material evidence from the prosecutor," *Gibson v. Superintendent of New Jersey Department of Law and Public Safety*, 411 F.3d 427 (3d Cir. 2005), and "[s]everal circuits have recognized that police officers and other state actors may be liable under §1983 for failing to disclose exculpatory information to the prosecutor," *McMillian v. Johnson*, 88 F.3d 1554, 1567 (11th Cir. 1996), amended 101 F.3d 1363 (11th Cir. 1996); *Walker v. City of New York*, 974 F.2d 293, 299 (2d Cir. 1992); *Geter v. Fortenberry*, 849 F.2d 1550, 1559 (5th Cir. 1988) quoting Gibson @ 443.

While examining what has transpired on this subject since the early 1960s, the Chief should first understand what the court decided in *Brady v. Maryland*[27] and why it is such an important case. Given the facts before the U.S. Supreme Court, Defendant Brady went to trial and was already convicted of murder, a crime Brady admitted he was involved in, but he denied he was the one who committed the murder. Actually, it was Brady's pre-conviction position that an accomplice was the murderer and, unbeknownst to Brady at the time, the accomplice admitted to committing the murder. The admission was not known to Brady, because his attorney's request for the accomplice's statements was not honored by the prosecutor. Coupling Brady's position with the accomplice's admission would have, in all likelihood, modified Brady's fate. In response to the facts, the Justices held prosecutors in a federal criminal case are required to disclose, on request of the defense, any known evidence even if favorable to the accused (i.e., "the suppression by the prosecution of evidence favorable to an accused upon request violates due process where the evidence is material either to guilt or to punishment, irrespective of the good faith or bad faith of the prosecution." *Id.* at 87). As such, Defendant Brady, if not for the Brady decision, would have ended like all other cases with similar facts: Favorable evidence known to the prosecutor being unfairly and unreasonably withheld in violation of a defendant's constitutional Due Process rights under the *Fifth* and *Fourteenth Amendments*.

---

[27] 373 U.S. 83 (1963)

Successful establishment of a *Brady* claim requires three findings:

(1) that evidence was suppressed.
(2) that this evidence was favorable to the accused.
(3) that the evidence was material either to guilt or punishment.

Brogdon v. Blackburn, 790 F.2d 1164, 1167 (5th Cir. 1986) (per curiam), *cert. denied*, 481 U.S. 1042, 107 S.Ct. 1985, 95 L.Ed.2d 824 (1987), quoting *Smith v. Black*, 904 F.2d 950, 963 (5th Cir. 1990). Logically, "material evidence" is evidence that if available and/or presented, in all probability, would have changed the outcome of the case.[28]

Furthermore, material evidence under *Brady* must be:

(1) in the possession of the prosecution.
(2) material
(3) exculpatory."[29]

In opposition to material evidence is material that even if available and/or presented would have no effect on the case's outcome (e.g., evidence viewed as neutral[30]). Failure to comply with *Brady*, commonly known now as a "Brady violation," could result in, for example, a new trial or reversal on appeal.

On or about nine years after *Brady*, the court held in *Giglio v. United States*, 405 U.S. 150, 154–55 (1972), that "when the reliability of a given witness may well be determinative of guilt or innocence, nondisclosure of evidence affecting credibility falls within the general rule of *Brady*." In other words, the government has a duty to bring forward any exculpatory information that would call into question the witnesses the government presents. These governmental witnesses include, but are certainly not limited to, law enforcement officers and although the importance of an officer's credible testimony has not and did not change, the disclosure of any and all exculpatory information related to the officer who is a witness did. It is here where the internal affairs investigator should remain aware that the kinds of issues that may draw immediate concern for a prosecution witness's credibility are, for

---

[28] See *United States v. Bagley*, 473 U.S. 667, 682 (1985).

[29] *United States v. Bhutani*, 175 F.3d 572, 577 (7th Cir. 1999); i.e., material evidence in this case came to light *after* the trial; thus, not a Brady violation.

[30] See *United States v. Rhodes*, 569 F.2d 384, 388 (2nd Cir. 1978), ("The inference to be drawn from this testimony was of a neutral nature").

example, authoring false police reports or conduct that involves moral turpitude or dishonesty. Appropriately, when it comes down to a police officer's credibility, sworn ethical officers who possess unimpeachable integrity take the position that they have nothing to hide, therefore, they hide nothing. Therefore, when an officer serves as a governmental witness, it is the officer's testimony that becomes material and if the officer's credibility is in doubt then by all means the incredible behavior could be potentially exculpatory, which warrants it's disclosure to the defense.

It should be noted that all too many times police officers are initially charged by their Chiefs with dishonesty based on the credible evidence collected during the investigation that is later dismissed through a plea deal or last-chance agreement. Cautiously, the Chief and internal affairs commander should be mindful of the possibility that just because the dishonesty charge was dismissed or merged into another charge through the negotiated settlement, it does not automatically mean it will not be eventually disclosed under *Brady*. The fact of the matter is, in the scenario described, the dishonesty count did not go away through a finding of non-sustained, unfounded, or exonerated. With this outcome, the dishonesty charge was never actually resolved in the officer's favor; therefore, the possibility exists that a defense attorney will be successful in gaining access to the internal affairs file in an attempt to impeach the credibility of the government's witness. More so, the chief and internal affairs investigator may be called at a future time to explain the dishonesty allegation, investigation, and underlying basis for the charges that were dismissed instead of being adjudicated.

Decades after *Brady*, a case went before the U.S. Supreme Court in which the prosecutor did not disclose information about a victim's guilty pleas that would have been favorable to the defendant. This exculpatory evidence was not disclosed, because the defense attorney, unlike in *Brady*, did not make a request. Rightly so and in full fairness to the defense, the court opined in *United States v. Agurs*, 427 U.S. 97 (1976) that just because the defendant did not request the disclosure of any and all material issues associated with the case, the prosecutor has a duty to disclose exculpatory information. They further held, "[i]f the omitted evidence creates a reasonable doubt that did not otherwise exist, constitutional error has been committed. This means that the omission must be evaluated in the context of the entire record. If there is no reasonable doubt about guilt whether or not the additional evidence is considered, there is no justification for a new trial. On the other hand, if the verdict is already of questionable validity, additional evidence of relatively minor importance might be sufficient to create a reasonable doubt." *Id.* at 112–13. Taking *Brady* and *Agurs* one step further, in 1995 the U.S. Supreme Court held that "the individual prosecutor has a duty to learn of any favorable evidence known to the others acting on the government's behalf in the case, including the police," *Kyles v. Whitley*, 514 U.S. 419, 437.

Reading into *Kyles*, it seems reasonable to conclude the Chief and internal affairs investigator also have an obligation, as the central depository of all confidentially held police disciplinary records, that they will be responsible parties and provide the prosecutor with any and all such Brady material in the officer's files. As the keepers of the files and the ones to disclose an officer's exculpatory evidence within those files to the prosecutor, would be questioned where the Chief and internal affairs investigator's liability if something is not disclosed that would be of material issue. And given that law enforcement officers have "an affirmative duty to intercede on the behalf of a citizen whose constitutional rights are being violated in his presence by other officers," *O'Neill v. Krzeminski*, 839 F.2d 9, 11 (2d Cir. 1988), then could the "presence" be the failure of the Chief's and internal affairs investigator's lack of knowing or knowing and not disclosing an officer's filing of a false police report or conduct that involves moral turpitude or dishonesty be stretched into a civil suit? While this issue to my knowledge has not been raised, *yet*, what is known is that liability does attach to those public officials who violate a citizen's constitutional rights (see *Monell v. Department of Social Services of New York*, 436 U.S. 658 (1978)) when policies are unconstitutionally implemented; therefore:

To put the disclosure issue into perspective, it is not inconceivable for a police officer to have a sustained charge of falsifying a police report and/or lying in one department to soon thereafter be hired by another department. Although the outgoing department rids themselves of a potential liability and an ineffective officer, the incoming department sometimes unsuspectedly gains the problem. Whether by ignorance on the officer's part or by chance, the officer's previous internal affairs file and discipline will only be released on the rarity of a court order resulting in any true disclosure of prior offenses to remain concealed. Because the offending officer does not reveal the discipline to the prosecutor and the incoming police department does not know about the officer's sustained offense from the outgoing department, nothing is revealed to the prosecutor. From there with the prosecutor innocently not being made aware of any offense, he would not be responsible to reveal something he is not aware of; thus, leaving the defense without the knowledge that there may be actual exculpatory evidence in existence that may be favorable to an arrestee who may actually be innocent and not even arrested if not for the sole actions of the dishonest officer. And while the non-disclosure can go years, possibly his entire career, if and when the right unrelenting and meticulous defense attorney eventually successfully exposes the officer's past, the department may be liable for their negligent hiring practices and the officer may be liable for his failure to disclose known information.

To limit the liability of the incoming department (i.e., which literally means every police agency), the application should contain a section on the acknowledgment of prior discipline and the release of any and all potentially exculpatory information. Additionally, the candidate should be required, as a prerequisite to being hired, to waive in writing the unfettered review of all previous disciplinary records where the officer was a target. This includes all discipline regardless of the complainant and the final disposition.

Additionally, there should be a written zero tolerance policy making it absolutely clear to every single law enforcement officer that sustained findings of dishonesty will result in immediate termination from the department. Furthermore, for those officers who, for whatever reasons, were not terminated and doing so now would be civilly unreasonable, there needs to be a policy that compels every sworn officer to disclose to the prosecutor any potentially exculpatory evidence. By potential, the evidence would include, but not be limited to, sustained as well as non-sustained offenses and the notified prosecutors should not be limited to just those involving criminal defendants. Besides the implementation of a well-written policy, the department should conduct in-service training with their officers on this policy, as well as all others, no less than annually. Once trained and retrained, the officers should sign a *Statement of Understanding* and make it part of the officer's training file.

As discussed with regards to an officer's files, the police department should have only one file that stores everything related to criminal investigations. Maintaining only one file guarantees the prosecutor will receive all relevant documents related to the investigation; thus, providing reinforcement to the prosecutor that no Brady material can be overlooked, missed, or mistakenly placed in an unofficial file instead.

Finally, with the internal affairs commander already acutely aware of any and all discipline involving every police officer within the agency, regardless of its nature, if and when a department chooses not to terminate an officer who is dishonest, it should be incumbent on the offending officer to report directly to the commander in writing all notifications made to the prosecutor along with the case number. These types of notification should be in writing and signed off as received by the prosecutor for each and every case involving the officer in question.

Chapter 17
Identifying Deceptive Behavior

Sigmund Freud said, "He that has eyes to see and ears to hear may convince himself that no mortal can keep a secret. If his lips are silent, he chatters with his fingertips; betrayal oozes out of him from every pore," and Charles Darwin said, "Repressed emotion almost always comes to the surface in some form of body motion," and "The stronger the emotional or stress response we are experiencing, the harder it is for us to censor it from the view of an observer." A practiced and dedicated internal affairs investigator should remember Freud and Darwin's famous quotes before, during, and after the assignment of a case.

Besides remembering the substance behind these famous quotes, a skilled investigator through his training and unending practice should employ identifying deceptive behavior techniques. The investigator going into an investigation knowing that 'people mean what they say and say what they mean' will likely uncover more than they initially anticipated. For those unfamiliar with the deceptive behavior practice, there are seminars conducted on deceptive behavior in written statements (e.g., "Statement Analysis") and seminars conducted on deceptive behavior through verbal statements (e.g., "Identifying Deceptive Behavior on a Traffic Stop") that every internal affairs investigator should attend.

Starting with some basics, investigators should make some obvious observations: like the head is the easiest for a person to control and the farther a body part from the person's head the harder its movement is to control (with the hardest to control being a person's eyes).

In abbreviated review of techniques, an investigator first needs to accept that their personal biases (e.g., age, ethnicity, family, friends, divorce, education, sex, etc.) unfortunately can influence an investigator's interpretation of a clue; however, for the most part, these influences are minuscule, because the investigator starts with a target officer's normal behavior. Additionally, these personal biases are negligent because the investigator focuses on not one clue but a cluster of clues. This is relevant because not one single clue or cluster, carries any more weight than another clue or cluster, and an investigator should not pay special attention using only one of his senses but should pay extra special attention using all of his applicable senses (i.e., sight, smell, taste, touch, and hearing). The more cues from the discussed categories below would ultimately mean the more the credibility behind his statement is diminished.

To establish norms, investigators should ask nonthreatening questions (e.g., full name, date of birth, education, etc.) and observe the target officer's supposedly unstressed reaction that will occur in a three- to five-second time frame of the initial question(s), keeping in mind that on or about 65 percent of a person's communications comes through by way of one's body language versus only about 7 percent that is vocal. Non-threatening questions are those questions that the target officer should know the answers to without the need to think or pause first before answering. A delayed response to these baseline questions would certainly be suspicious, but of course it may just serve as a sign of nervousness depending on the type and kind of investigation as well as his role in the allegations under investigation.

Lying vs. Deception

We know at times that people lie about money (to make them look more successful) or lie about running into a traffic jam so that they won't have to admit to oversleeping. These lies are tempting options sometimes spontaneously offered on a moment's notice to help cover up other behaviors or outcomes the person is not comfortable with telling outright. These types of lies are blatantly untrue statements and can be proven false by the investigator (e.g., can prove how much the person makes and can prove if there was a traffic jam). A liar creates an untrue statement, puts it out there for the receiver, and assumes (or hopes) nobody will double check its accuracy. While a lie is an unmistakable false statement able to be proved, a deceptive statement is intended to mislead the receiver.

There are several ways a target officer can mislead the investigator; for example, they can avoid the issue (e.g., question) or they can omit the truth from their response. On the other hand, the investigator will conscientiously allow the target to deceive him by simply not questioning the accuracy of the target's statement. In actuality, a lie is merely a form of deception; whereby, a lie is aggressive, open, and able to be proved, a deceptive statement is passive-aggressive, confined, and will need further examination that a seasoned investigator will actively pursue and a new investigator should learn to look deeper into.

When a target officer tells a lie, he realizes his lie has the ability to be analyzed, attacked, and proven to be false—thus, the possibility a departmental investigation could turn criminal. Therefore, even a hardened liar will resort to some form of deception instead of lying because the target knows his response will be presented with indistinctness and will not lock him into unarguable facts. The target officer realizes their deceptive statement, on the surface, is satisfactory enough with most investigators, but vague enough to give the officer the ability to redirect should the need arise.

When truthful people answer questions it would be reasonable to accept that their answers are quick, direct, and to the point. Furthermore, they are not afraid to offer theories and are willing to provide reasons why they are innocent of the allegations before them; deceptive people, however, make excuses before, during or after the interview. Someone being deceptive also displays a bad memory of the alleged events or anything surrounding the incident in question; they defend their answers with small immaterial details; and are generally slow to answer. Hence, just as honest people are generally relaxed and open, dishonest people are not; thus, displaying even mild forms of tension, nervousness, and distant or hollow stares. When comparing the target officer's normal behavior (i.e., baseline), the investigator should look for isolated symptoms such as fidgeting, rapid speech, a change in voice (e.g., pitch, volume, tone), nervousness, and licking lips and teeth. That is, an investigator needs to pay special attention to a target officer's normal behavior to notice any deviations because symptoms may not be significant, but when a target is telling the truth his manner should not notably or suddenly change.

An acceptable truism in human nature tends to leave people with an overpowering need to tell others what they know. This can be seen through the swiftness you repeat, or a friend repeats, intimate and personal information even though you were told or you told him or her "don't tell anyone, this is just between you and me." The fact of the matter is, everything that crosses a person's lips is done so through choice or accident; therefore, the specific words used, even if they seem insignificant or unrelated to the discussion, should be treated as significant and related (i.e., each word means something even if the sender and receiver do not realize it at the time).

Remember, no single clue or cluster (e.g., verbal or nonverbal) will point to one's truthfulness or deceptiveness, and an investigator needs to establish a baseline first and then look for any changes in the target officer's behavior. For example, when asked a question look for what is missing from his answer (i.e., lies through omission) or insertions in the response that are not consistent with the rest of the answer (i.e., lies through addition). Excluding those with a speech impediment, the investigator should find it noteworthy when an officer stalls in answering a question as this could represent the need to organize his thoughts first instead of offering an answer through memory, or he goes through a process in his thoughts of figuring out just how much he can say without going from deceptiveness to a lie. Other stalling methods include, but are not limited to, laughing before answering, coughing, and one of the most common is answering a question with a question. It is reasonable to assume that stalling would occur more times with a deceptive answer versus a truthful one.

Before or during an investigatory interview, the investigator should document not only the answers to directed questions but also any comments over and above what seem out of place. Some of the notable interruptions include a target officer focusing on a finite error in an investigator's question, but disregarding the question as a whole; complaining and/or threatening to gain the investigator's sympathy or poorly attempt to instill fear; claims of being ill or coming down with something that would prevent him from continuing with the interview; announcing he is under a doctor's care or taking prescription medicine; being overly polite, complimenting the investigator and/or his skills; and inappropriately interrupting the process.

Other verbal insertions the investigator should take notice of are words like: ah, err, um, and uh. The target officer may also swallow more than observed during normal behavior, which could be used as a stalling technique and a sign of stress. Additionally, while focusing on inserted words, the investigator should pay special attention to missing suffixes (e.g., … ing; … ed; … es; etc.) and common words used to make a complete sentence (e.g., the; and; or; etc.).

I Don't Recall

Frequently encouraged by their representatives, it is all too common for target officers to respond to questions with phrases like, "I don't remember"; "I don't recall"; and "Not that I can think of." While using these phrases for questions the target really does not recall or remember is appropriate. However, when officers use these types of phrases they may have avoided answering one question, but depending on the circumstances could have raised other more serious concerns. For example, police officers' memories are essential in being hired and continuing to work in law enforcement. Police officers are constantly put in a position where they need to remember faces, names, statements, incidents, and events as they unfold on traffic stops, investigations, and arrests. An officer's memory and the recalling of the preceding examples are crucial for courtroom testimony, especially when many times they are not called on to testify for months and possibly years later.

Alarming to an internal affairs investigator when the target officer responds all too frequently and continually with "I do not recall" type answers to incidents that occurred only hours, days, or weeks earlier raises reasonable suspicion as to whether or not this target officer continues to be fit for duty. In preparation for an upcoming administrative investigation, it is highly suggested the investigator retrieve several open investigations and summonses that pre-date the incident under investigation and as the target officer responds to questions with "I do not recall" answers, the investigator should than question the target on his memory with regards to those open investigations. If the target has the ability to recall events in the one but not the other, this would warrant further examination as to the truthfulness of the "I do not recall" answers versus the target officer's short- and long-term memory.

But

Incidentally, as Dr. Phil tells his audience, anything after a "but" undermines whatever comes before; therefore, it is important for the investigator to acknowledge the discounted comment before the overriding comment that follows. In opposition to the word "but," investigators should pay closer attention to such phrases as "by the way" and "one more thing," because it is beyond happenstance that what comes next out through the target's lips will be important to him.

125 out of 500

When linking words to the thoughts of the speaker, it is important to grasp that people generally are able to run through their minds approximately four times more words each minute than they are able to speak. Bearing this in mind, what the target officer wants to tell the investigator sometimes is mixed with his thoughts he actually wanted to remain buried (i.e., Freudian slips). It is these "slips" that the investigator should be spending time on because while they may seem insignificant to most, they are very significant to an investigation and about the target's conscious unspoken thoughts.

Other important principles regarding verbal communications include the obvious handicap of someone to forget more rapidly a made-up story versus a truthful one from memory; therefore, asking the target officer to repeat an answer to an earlier question or to provide the details of the incident in reverse could be telling. Disclaimers like "I know this sounds strange" are also red flags because the target officer does not believe himself what he's about to disclose.

To be fair, most people have a difficult time lying and will not lie; knowing this, the investigator should go into the investigation without the assumption the target is lying, but as discussed above they may not tell you everything they know, anything incriminating, or will hold back crucial or damaging information. As a result, it would obviously be in the investigator's best interest to listen to what the target's saying, because rarely will a guilty officer state "I did not do it." Instead, the guilty officer will dance around the question or resort to some form of deception and as a last resort he will lie.

"I know" vs. "I think" vs. "I believe"

There is a difference between the three words: know, believe, and think and the investigator should know what those differences are. In the order of reliability, if a target officer claims to *know* something it normally means that he has direct knowledge about the thing in question he is discussing. When a target officer states he *believes* it normally means he does not have a direct knowledge about what's under discussion, but that he is close enough to the matter that he emotionally has faith in what he says to be accurate. Lastly, *think* is the lowest form of confidence the target officer has in the claim he is presenting. While using the word "think" does not necessarily mean the target officer is being deceptive, it does mean the investigator, depending on the question asked and the answer provided as it relates to the investigation's relevance, needs to explore his answer in more depth. For example: I *know* what I did was in violation of the policy versus I *believe* what I did was in violation of the policy versus I *think* what I did was in violation of the policy. Obviously, the target officer admitting he knew what he did was in violation of the policy will have more weight than his just believing it to be or even less his thinking it was wrong. Thus, *knowing* he's in violation is enough to move on to the next question, but his only *believing* or *thinking* he's in violation would require subsequent questions to lock him in. (Remember, "notice" is the first step for "just cause" and without notice the case is more than likely fatally flawed.)

Non-Verbal Communication

As discussed, the target officer's immediate and initial response is important to the internal affairs investigator and cannot be overlooked, but an investigator's ability to pick up on these sometimes split-second non-verbal clues will take continual practice. Today with reality television (e.g., "Big Brother") and game shows (e.g., "Friend or Foe"), investigators can practice their identifying deceptive skills each and every day, but practice cannot stop when the television goes off and can also be used on family members (e.g., works great when dealing with children) and friends.

Head

Starting with the head (the easiest body part to control) as Darwin stated, "A person listening to and interested in comments made by another often tilts the head to one side or the other"; hence, a reaction the investigator should be able to pick up on. (Did you ever talk to a dog and the dog tilts his head slightly? This is an example of the dog showing an interest in what the speaker has to say.) Another reaction, when compared to the target's norms, would be his having a greater number of touches to his head based.

Eyes

Any changes noticed in the target's normal eye contact should be noted if it is associated with a question including, but not limited to, normal patterns (e.g., unbroken eye contact to fragmented eye contact) and changes in direction (e.g., looking up changed to looking left, right, down or straight). On average, during most conversations, people maintain eye contact on or about 50% of the time; therefore, any significant deviation from this percentage should be noted especially if it differs from the target's normal eye contact.

Admittedly there are published studies discussing the direction of a person's eyes in relationship to giving a truthful answer versus a deceptive one, this will not be explored within; however, looking for the target officer's three whites ("San Paku"—spiritually unwell) of his eyes (i.e., white on the bottom, to the right, and to the left of the pupil) could indicate the target officer does not have confidence in what he is saying and/or confidence in what he is saying is going to be believed. Also, the investigator should take notice any color changes or constricting of the target's pupils.

Eyelids

Extended closures of the target's eyelids could be a sign of stress and excessive blinking could be a sign of rapid thinking, but if the blinking comes to a near halt it could indicate the target is in deep thought. Obviously these are in comparison to the target's normal eyelid movements.

Eyebrows

"... both eyebrows raised high along with the mouth slightly open, the subject is experiencing shock or surprise" (Darwin, 1872), implying the target did not expect the question presented and may have been caught off-guard.

Nose

Along with the head, a person under stress will more than likely touch their nose in greater frequency. This is because a person's nose is one of the most stress sensitive parts of a person's body.

Mouth

Watch for yawning as a sign of stress or used to delay a response. Other signs related to the mouth worth picking up on are biting on fingernails or any objects (e.g., pen, hair).

Arms / Hands

A study followed by independent tests has shown that when a person folds their right arm over their left arm they are dominant and controlling while those who fold their left arm over their right arm are passive. This is important to determine before an investigatory interview, because it could be valuable when forming questions and the investigator's initial approach.

Less movement of one's hands or arms tends to imply decep-tiveness, but also does keeping arms staunchly to one's side, in their pockets, and clenched. Further observations should see if the fingers are open or closed and if the arms are crossed against the chest, which is symbolically used as a barrier between him and you.

Phraseology

How questions are phrased are important to any good internal affairs investigation and should be reviewed carefully before presenta-tion. Given the goal of an internal affairs investigation is to get to the facts, asking the questions in person or in writing should be of no difference in accomplishing the mission.

For the most part, questions should not be compound since compound questions certainly make it easier for the target officer to avoid giving a direct response. A compound question is one that asks more than one thing in one single question (e.g., Did you text and phone the victim?; thus, a "yes" response would need to be further clarified as to whether he texted, phoned or both). Additionally, probing questions should not be specific or to the point (e.g., "Was the car red?" versus "Tell me what color the car was."), because specific questions lead the target's answer in only one direction and offers the target possibly more information than he possessed before the question was asked (e.g., he may not have known the car was red before the question was asked). Another thing this type of question does is give the target an answer from within the question (e.g., if the car is red, he may now know more information than he had before the investigator asked the question).

In remembering that everything the target says has meaning, an investigator should use the art of silence to his advantage. If you recall, the target is thinking many more words than he can speak in one minute, when an investigator is silent, the target's mind is still in a thought and it is not uncommon for him to add more if the investigator takes a long pause. Another valuable tool the investigator could use is the word "... and ..." once the target finishes answering a question. The use of the word "and" gives the target the ability to express further what he was thinking.

An investigator should never ask "why" and when listening to the target's response he should pay close attention to the consistency of the pronouns (e.g., we, us, they) used (e.g., using "me" in one sentence and "us" in another; thus, adding others into the scenario who the investigator may not have known about or "I left my hat" versus "I left the hat"—could be a sign he is trying to distance himself from his hat or the hat is not his). Using the pronoun "my" links the item to the individual, but using "the" does not and may require further examination. Additionally, when a target responds with "you know" it is important to sort through his response to make certain he is talking about himself in his response and is not an attempt to put his words in the investigator's mouth or mind. When the phrase "you know" is used, the target is trying to shift his knowledge (or lack thereof) to the investigator; thus, weakening his responsibility.

For example, "You know how nobody in the department ..." accomplishes at least three things:

(1) Introduces an automatic defense for the target;

(2) Invites a practice into the department that may not have existed before; and

(3) Cleverly makes the target the cat and the investigator the mouse as it relates to this specific question and answer, including anything else that unravels off of it.

Verb Tenses

Listening to how the target answers a direct question could be telling if the question was asked in a generic sense, but answered specifically. For example, "Did you ever drive the police car out of town?" and he answers "I didn't drive Car-54 out of town." His response is in the present tense and specifically Car-54 while the question asked was in reference to every moment before the question was asked and was about all police cars, not just the one he narrowed his answer down to. Considering investigations are not related to incidents that did not happen yet, questions are asked in the past tense; therefore, all answers should also be answered in the same fashion.

Order

Listen to the order in which names or items are listed, because the order probably comes with a deeper meaning worth exploring, depending on the investigation. If the target officer lists other officers involved in an incident, he may be listing them in the order of their involvement or his relationship with them. Depending on the type of investigation, interviewing the last named person first may prove fruitful, because the first named person probably has more involvement in the incident than the others from the perspective of the target officer.

Chronological Order

Recall by memory is normally presented in chronological order; therefore, when questioned on an incident it would be expected for the description of events to be presented in order to the investigator. If, however, the description is not in chronological order it is possible the answer is not by memory or words may be added for effect. This sequence is picked up by a good investigator, and when a target makes up things as he goes along he will occasionally forget what he stated earlier. Our lives are set up to be lived in chronological order; therefore, it makes sense that our memory when reviewing events will be presented the same way. If the events are not presented as such it could lead the investigator to wonder: If they do not live their lives that way, why are they recalling events that way?

When the answers do not freely flow, something is probably amiss: Either something is omitted or added, but the investigator should be cognizant to the fact that very few people will be able to tell a historical story verbatim, and when their story is abbreviated it is assumed things will be left out. In light of the fact that the investigator will have the entire case investigated before questioning the target, if this happens, the investigator should be able to compare the facts gathered to the answers provided and determine what pieces are missing and how significant those missing pieces are. If significant enough, the investigator would need to examine his answers further.

Answering Questions

When the target does not want to answer a question or provide certain information they will attempt to not answer. They will either do this through answering partially, answering a question with a question, or using the stalling techniques discussed previously. Obviously, if the target does not answer the question, the chances he is trying to hide something are highly probable; therefore, those questions the target tries to avoid should be the questions the investigator explores further. Furthermore, for tactical purposes, phrase all questions as if you, the investigator, already know the answer. (Remember the target officer does not know what you know.) That is, even when it is believed the target officer will not lie or be deceptive, asking assumptive questions will elicit a much more revealing response (e.g., "Did you go to the bar after work?" versus "Tell me what time you went to the bar after work?" or "Why were you late this morning?" versus "Tell me how late you were this morning?").

Closing

In closing, every investigator should be trained in Statement Analysis and some form of Identifying Deceptive Behavior. Even with superficial training or a close review of the material presented above, the investigator should be able to start to look for some of the cues/clusters in determining whether or not the target officer is downright lying or some form of deception is noted through the target's verbal and non-verbal communication. Obviously, if and when any doubt exists the investigator needs to take the safest course of action and err on the side of caution. In order to become proficient, the investigator needs to continually practice, pay attention, and listen to exactly what is being said.

Chapter 18
After the Investigation

The Chief of Police should be the sole disciplinarian for the members of his department. *Anything else could generally do four things:*

(1) Undermine the authority of the Chief in the eyes of the union,

(2) Shows a distrust for the Chief of Police,

(3) Could pit the chief against the other individual(s) who have the authority to override the Chief's decision,

(4) Chips away at department morale, and

(5) The union will use any dissension to their advantage and has the potential to become a political issue; thus taking the focus off of the discipline and on the discord between the chief and his higher authority.

More so, the Chief as the department head should be given the full authority to oversee the day-to-day operations of the police department without interference. Running the day-to-day operations needs to include the authority to discipline his force and its officers and personnel in the best interest of the public entity. Just as nobody knows the intimacies of an investigation like the internal affairs investigator, nobody knows what it is like to be the chief until they are actually the chief; therefore, those not familiar with the intricacies, culture, and subculture of the police agency should rely on their department head to make the right and many times very difficult decisions.

Once an investigation is deemed completed by the internal affairs investigator and turned over to the Chief a determination is made as to whether or not charges are appropriate based on the sufficiency of the information gathered. (If, for whatever reason, the Chief after reviewing the investigation believes there is not sufficient information to render a fair and reasonable decision as to appropriate charges, it is incumbent on the Chief to return the insufficient and incomplete investigation back to the internal affairs investigator and insist on nothing less than a thorough, accurate, and complete investigation in return.)

Once the Chief is satisfied he possesses a thorough, accurate, and complete investigation and has sufficient information to file the appropriate charges against the target officer, he should take administrative action on those confirmed violations as swiftly as possible and with minimal delay. In most circumstances, it is not the decision to file the charges based on the investigator's findings that delays the case from moving forward quickly, but it is the decision on what is the appropriate penalty in relationship to the charges. The fact of the matter is, the hardest decision to make in relationship to an internal affairs investigation is coming to a fair and just penalty to impose based on the charges filed.

Prior to the protection plans as discussed above, the Chief for the most part would impose a penalty he believed was fair and just based on the charges. Then, if the target officer or union agreed with the findings and penalty, the parties once in agreement would sign a consent agreement and the agreed-upon penalty would be carried out. However, since the inception of the protection plans the game changed and now even if the target officer and union officials agree with the investigator's findings, they still hire an attorney to contest the entire process from allegation to preliminary notice of charges. Right, wrong, or indifferent, this game change impacted the Chief's decision on the counts and penalty, because in order to get to a fair and just settlement now the counts may be increased, which ultimately will augment the penalty. To put these practices in understandable terms in years past the Chief would file one or two charges against the target with a two-day penalty that the target and union accepted as reasonable; however, now to get to the same two-day suspension the Chief may need to file additional counts against the target that increase the penalty. Those additional charges could have been filed in the first case as well, but the Chief did not file those charges because in the end he only wanted a two-day suspension and without the protection plans he ultimately would have ended up with the two-day suspension. Now, about the same two-day suspension—the taxpayers are also compelled to hire an attorney to negotiate the settlement with the target officer's attorney versus years ago when the Chief negotiated the identical results with the union. Unfortunately, what the game change also created are Chiefs handing out an inflated penalty (e.g., demotion, termination) to force the target and his attorney into negotiations. Even as this practice on the surface appears unreasonable, it is actually in place to save the taxpayers the burden of spending tax dollars unnecessarily to eventually come to the same results. In comparison, the above saves the protection plan from excessive and unnecessary attorney and expert witness fees that they would have spent going to trial.

That said, once served with the preliminary notice of charges and proposed penalty the officer should be given three options:

(1) Pleads guilty to the charges and accepts the penalty as filed;

(2) Pleads not guilty, or

(3) Pleads guilty to the charges, but wants to present mitigating factors on behalf of the penalty.

Obviously, if the officer selects option number one, the Chief, through the internal affairs investigator, would notify the officer in writing, execute the penalty, and fittingly update the officer's personnel file. If the officer chooses option number three, the officer, union representative, or attorney would present their position with respect to the penalty; and once a decision is finalized, the procedure as expressed in option number one would be uniformly followed. However, if the officer picks option number two and he is entitled to a hearing either through statute, case law, or the officer's collective bargaining agreement, the internal affairs unit would make the arrangements including, but not limited to, providing discovery; confirming the date, hiring a prosecutor; hiring a hearing officer; and securing witnesses for live testimony.

Hearing

Where a law, regulation, or agreement exists that warrants a hearing based on the degree of the penalty imposed, before the penalty can be carried out to not "deprive any person of life, liberty, or property, without due process of law,"[31] the charged officer is entitled to be heard before an impartial hearing officer. If, however, after a review of the evidence in support of the charges there are no material facts in dispute, the hearing officer is afforded the ability to decide the case on the material presented. However, if a material fact is in dispute (which almost always is the case), the charged officer can with or without legal representation cross-examine any witnesses who may be called to testify against him and to present witnesses on his own behalf.

Once the parties rest, the hearing officer should render a decision on the filed charges of sustained or non-sustained and offer his suggestions with respect to an appropriate penalty on the sustained charges. The hearing officer should timely provide a copy of the decision to the

---

[31] U.S. Constitution, Amendment XIV.

charged officer or his attorney, the prosecutor, the Chief, and the internal affairs commander, unless policy dictates otherwise.

If the hearing officer's decision is final and not just a recommendation to the jurisdiction's appropriate or hiring authority, the Chief through the internal affairs commander should see that the penalty is carried out. If the hearing officer's decision is only a recommendation to the jurisdiction's appropriate or hiring authority, then the appropriate authority would review the hearing officer's recommendation and either accept or modify it to their satisfaction; whereby, the Chief would then, through the internal affairs commander, see that the penalty is carried out. From there, the commander should insure all the required forms are completed and the charged officer's internal affairs and personnel file are updated.

The internal affairs investigator should also send out thank you notices to all witnesses for their assistance and the agency's appreciation for their time and consideration to the matter. Finally, to close out the jacket, the internal affairs investigator should send a letter to the complainant, if any, with the resolution of the allegation. This letter should be void of any confidential information not lawfully permitted to be released to the public. A copy of the complainant's final letter and all witness letters should be made part of the internal affairs file.

White Sheet

Anytown Police Department
OFFICIAL REPORT

TO: The subject officer(s) shall return the completed
                                       White Sheet to the assigned supervisor no later
                                       than six (6) hours after the start of their very
FROM: next shift.

DATE:

SUBJECT:

YOUR RESPONSE SHALL BE **IN YOUR HANDWRITING** WITH YOUR INITIALS
AND DATE IN **BLUE** INK NEXT TO EACH ANSWER.

PLEASE ATTACH ALL SUPPORTIVE DOCUMENTS YOU WISH TO BE
CONSIDERED WITH REGARDS TO THIS INVESTIGATION.

Specifically, narrowly, and directly answer the following:

1. **ALWAYS SECOND TO LAST QUESTION:** If there's any information,
    surrounding this investigation, that you know or knew [directly or
    indirectly] that hasn't been asked and/or answered, please provide
    it now. (Note: You must provide a response—N/A is NOT AN
    ACCEPTABLE RESPONSE)

Anytown Police Department
OFFICIAL REPORT

2. **ALWAYS LAST QUESTION:** Please confirm that every question answered, regarding this investigation, is everything that you know or knew [directly or indirectly] surrounding this investigation. (Note: You must provide a response—N/A is NOT AN ACCEPTABLE RESPONSE) [An example of an acceptable response could be "yes" or "no."]

If you need additional space, please continue on a separate sheet of paper; however, you are required to affix your signature and date in blue ink to all attached sheets. This is not inclusive, further questions may be forthcoming

Falsification to authorities. "A person commits a crime if he makes a written false statement which he does not believe to be true; therefore, I solemnly swear that all statements made are the truth, the whole truth, and nothing but the truth to the effect that false statements made therein are punishable."

Signed: _____ Official Title: _____ Date: _____

Use the space provided, then, if you need additional space, please continue on a separate sheet of paper; however, you are required to affix your signature and date in blue ink to all attached sheets.

Appendix B

Police Officer Responsibilities Checklist

POLICE OFFICER RESPONSIBILITIES CHECKLIST

_____ Under the supervision of the Chief of Police performs law enforcement work involving the protection of life and property through the enforcement of laws and related preventive and investigative work.

_____ Under the supervision of the Chief of Police performs law enforcement work involving the protection of life and property through the enforcement of laws and related preventive and investigative work.

_____ Provides assistance to the general public, such as for lock-outs of homes and motor vehicles, deliver emergency messages, assist the sick and infirm.

_____ Answer calls and complaints involving drunkenness, domestic disputes, fires, thefts, accidents, and other misdemeanors and felonies.

_____ Conduct preliminary investigations, gathers evidence, makes arrests, and testifies in court, serves court papers.

_____ Answers telephones receiving complaints, inquiries, and requests for police assistance. Secures information as to the nature and location of offense or accident.

_____ Searches for and collects evidence. Seeks and develops sources of information. Ascertains information necessary for the arrest of person alleged to have committed a crime. Participates in the searching and booking of persons arrested. Prepares and types reports and maintains records.

_____ Directs traffic. Operates radar equipment. Enforces municipal regulations. Issues citations. Ensures operational effectiveness of a variety of police and first-aid equipment.

145

_____ Conducts accident investigations, provides first-aid for the injured, and takes safeguards to prevent further accident. Interview principals and witnesses, taking written statements. Examine vehicles and roadways, observing traffic control devices and obstructions to view. Observes and reports all required information concerning accident.

_____ Investigates crimes. Searches for and preserves evidence. Interrogates suspects and witnesses. Maintains surveillance over persons and places suspected of illegal operations. Fingerprints prisoners and photographs persons arrested for crimes.

_____ Serves as assigned as a police dispatcher.

_____ Performs related work as required.

Appendix C
Verification of Illness Form

LAST NAME: _____

REPORTING SICK PRIOR TO DUTY:

Date Called:_____ Time Called: _____ Day of Week: _____

Date Officer will be taking sick leave: _____Hours Scheduled: _____

Reason Officer is out sick: _____

Officer's Location while on Sick Leave: _____Phone Number: _____

Signature of On-Duty Shift Supervisor taking call: _____

      DOCTOR'S NOTE REQUIRED: YES _____   NO _____

REPORTING SICK, WHILE ON-DUTY

Date Officer Went Home: _____Officer will be absent: _____

Reason why Officer will be going home sick: _____

Officer's Location while on Sick Leave: _____Number: _____

Signature of On-Duty Shift Supervisor: _____

Officer will be at Doctor's or the equivalent from: _____ hours to _____hours

Officer will be voting from: _____hours to _____hours.

Officer will be attending religious services from: _____hours to _____ hours

Officer will be attending to a family emergency from: _____hours to ____hours

Documented by: _____

The Officer reporting sick leave will upon return to duty, review this document and by the act of affixing signature below attest that it is an accurate description of the circumstances causing his incapacitation on the date(s) shown above. The on-duty Shift Supervisor will witness the reporter's signature.

147

I have read the contents of this document and find them to be a true and accurate description of my reported illness.

Officer's signature: _____Date:_____

Shift Supervisor's signature: _____

Resources

Chapter 13

ADA Enforcement Guidance: "Preemployment Disability-Related Questions and Medical Examinations" (1995)

Fischler, Gary L., Ph.D. (2001). *Psychological Fitness-for-Duty Examinations: Practical Considerations for Public Safety Departments.* Minneapolis, MN: Illinois Law Enforcement Executive Forum

The Institute for Forensic Psychology, 5 Fir Court, Suite 2, Oakland, New Jersey 07436

Chapter 17

Adams, Susan H. "Statement Analysis: What Do Suspects Words Really Reveal?" *FBI Law Enforcement Bulletin* (2003).

Adams, Susan H, and John P. Jarvis. "Are You Telling Me The Truth." *FBI Law Enforcement Bulletin* (2004).

Berne, Eric. *Games People Play*. New York: Ballantine Books, 1996.

Dimitrius, Jo-Ellen, and Mark Mazzarella. *Reading People*. New York: Ballantine Books, 2008.

Hess, John E. *Interviewing and Interrogation for Law Enforcement*. 2nd ed. New Providence; Bender & Co., 2010.

Lewis, Jerry A. "Statement Analysis: The Truth Lies Within." 1 Jan. 2008. Training Course Material.

Liberman, David J. *Never Be Lied To Again*. New York: St. Martin's Griffin, 1999.

McClish, Mark. *I Know You Are Lying*. Winterville: The Marpa Group, 2001.

Nance, Jeff. *Conquering Deception*. Kansas City: Irvin Benham Group, 2001.

Sollars, Dale L. "Identifying Deceptive Behavior." 3 Feb. 2003. File last modified on 5 Feb. 2003. Training Course Material.

Vrij, Aldert. *Detecting Lies and Deceit*. New York: John Wiley & Sons, 2001.

Walters, Stan B. "Interviewing for Credibility: Accurate Identification of Deception Behaviors." *The Speaker Studio*. n.d. Web. 17 Mar. 2011. <http://www.thespeakerstudio.com/esources//_For_Credibility 1.htm>.

Walters, Stan B. *Principles of Kinesic Interview and Interrogation*. 2nd ed. Boca Raton: CRC Press, 2002.

Index